Understanding LEADERSHIP

Theories & Concepts
3rd Edition

C.B. Crawford, Ph.D
Curtis L. Brungardt, Ph.D
Micol Maughan, Ph.D
FORT HAYS STATE UNIVERSITY

Contributions and Foreward by Joseph D. Potts
UNIVERSITY OF KANSAS

Cover photograph Lighthouse copyright © Corbis Digital Stock

This custom textbook includes materials submitted by the Author for publication by John Wiley & Sons, Inc. The material has not been edited by Wiley and the Author is solely responsible for its content.

ISBN 978-0-471-72912-9

20 19 18 17 16 15 14 13

TABLE OF CONTENTS

Foreword

Preface

UNIT 1 – THE BASICS

Chapter 1 - Defining Leadership **3**

    Chapter Objectives 3

    Introduction 4

    A Brief Historical Overview 5

    Leadership vs. Management 7

    Myths of Leadership 9

    Summary 11

    References 12

    Discussion Questions 13

    Case Study 15

Chapter 2 - The History of Leadership **17**

    Chapter Objectives 17

    Introduction 18

    Tribal Leadership 18

    Pre-Classical Leadership 18

    Classical Leadership 19

    Progressive Leadership 20

    Post-Progressive Leadership 23

    Summary 23

    References 23

    Discussion Questions 25

    Activity 27

UNIT 2 - THEORIES OF LEADERSHIP

Chapter 3 - Trait Theories **31**

    Chapter Objectives 31

    Introduction.. 32

    Nature vs. Nurture... 32

    Earliest Theories... 33

    Stogdill's 1948 Review 33

    Stogdill's 1974 Review 34

    Charismatic Theories 35

    Contemporary Traits Approaches 36

    Summary... 38

    References.. 38

    Discussion Questions 39

    Activity 41

Chapter 4 - Behavioral Theories **43**

    Chapter Objectives 43

    Introduction.. 44

    Early Behavioral Approaches 44

    McGregor Theory X and Theory Y 47

    Two-Factor Approaches 48

    Summary... 51

    References.. 51

    Discussion Questions 53

    Activity 56

Chapter 5 - Contingency & Situational Theories **57**

    Chapter Objectives 57

    Introduction.. 58

    Fiedler's Contingency Model 58

    Path-Goal Theory 62

    Situational Leadership Model 64

    Summary... 66

    References.. 66

    Discussion Questions 67

    Case Study 69

Chapter 6 - Power and Influence Theories **71**

    Chapter Objectives 71

    Introduction 72

    Elements of Power 72

    Elements of Influence 77

    Summary 79

    References 79

    Discussion Questions 81

    Case Study 83

Chapter 7 - Transformational, Cultural, and Symbolic Theories **85**

    Chapter Objectives 85

    Introduction 86

    Transformational Leadership Theory 86

    Organizational Culture and Leadership 89

    Symbolic Leadership 91

    Summary 92

    References 92

    Discussion Questions 93

    Activity 95

UNIT 3 - CONTEMPORARY LEADERSHIP

Chapter 8 - The New Age of Leadership **99**

    Chapter Objectives 99

    Introduction 100

    A New Definition 100

    Leadership vs. Leader Development 101

    The Post-Industrial View 102

    Distributed Leadership 103

    Summary 104

    References 105

    Discussion Questions 107

    Case Study 109

Chapter 9 - Social Change Leadership **111**

Chapter Objectives 111

Introduction 112

Social Change Leadership Theory 112

Collaborative Leadership 114

The UCLA Model 116

Summary 117

References 117

Discussion Questions 119

Activity 122

Chapter 10 - Risk Leadership **123**

Chapter Objectives 123

Introduction 124

Antecedents of Risk Leadership 124

Risk Agents and the Risk Agency 126

The Process of Risk Leadership 127

Outcomes of Risk Leadership 129

Risk Leadership Cultures 130

Summary 131

References 132

Discussion Questions 133

Activity 135

Chapter 11 – Followership **137**

Chapter Objectives 137

Introduction 138

Emerging View of Followers 138

Behavioral Styles of Followers 140

The Courageous Follower 141

Servant Leadership, Shared Leadership,
& Followership 142

Summary 143

References 144

Discussion Questions 145

Activity 148

Chapter 12 - Leadership as Ethics 149

Chapter Objectives 149

Introduction 150

Leadership *and* Ethics 150

Leadership *as* Ethics 151

Leadership or Management? 152

Redefining Leadership 153

Summary 153

References 154

Discussion Questions 155

Activity 157

Chapter 13 - Leadership and Change Making 159

Chapter Objectives 159

Introduction 160

Characteristics of Change 160

Barriers to Change 161

Phases of the Change Process 161

Effective Change Agents 163

Summary 164

References 164

Discussion Questions 165

Activity 167

FOREWORD

Is Bill Gates a leader? Was Mahatma Gandhi a leader? Most students answer yes to both questions. If you did too, what would you say they have in common that makes them both leaders? If you said no, what do you see as the primary difference between them? The fact that you are reading this suggests that you have at least some interest in becoming a leader—or perhaps in becoming a better one. Do you hope to be more like Gates, more like Gandhi, or more like someone else entirely? Why?

Your answers to these and similar questions reveal a great deal about you, because leadership is an intensely personal activity. Your answers also reveal what you believe leadership is and should be. This book cannot change who you are as a person; that part is up to you. But the authors do hope that what you learn from this text will shape, add to, or correct your beliefs about leadership.

Herein you will encounter many different ways of thinking about this important topic. As you read and study this material, think carefully about the approach being taken in each chapter. Interestingly, you may come to the conclusion that some of the "theories of leadership" would be better classified as techniques or methods. Others, upon reflection, might seem to you to be forms or styles of management, rather than theories of leadership. Some may seem clearly to be theories in that they try to describe or explain the phenomenon of leadership, rather than present a new strategy or approach. You might conclude, for example, that the section on Joseph Rost presents an actual theory of leadership, but that empowerment is a technique, and that path-goal theory has to do with management instead of leadership. Or you might not.

Which concepts fall into which category? Ultimately, you must decide these things for yourself. As you go deeper in the study of leadership, you will find that different people mean many, many different things when they use the word "leadership." In fact, one of the most important contemporary scholars on the subject, Dr. Joanna Ciulla, argues that those who study leadership should not be worried about defining it in one particular way. But while this may be a defensible academic argument, it isn't very helpful to those who really want to lead. That is one thing that we can say for certain: leadership is practical—it is something people *do*. In order to learn to do something, or learn to do something better, we have to commit ourselves to a particular idea of what that thing is.

That is one good reason to carefully develop (or choose) your own definition of leadership. Here are two more. First, whether you like the idea or not, there will be many times in your life when you are not the one in charge. Until you have a clear idea of what leadership should be, you won't be able to evaluate the efforts or appeals of those you have the opportunity to follow. Second, there will be times when you are asked to help in the process of selecting others for leadership roles. You won't know whom to choose if you don't know what leaders are supposed to do.

Leadership is an exciting, challenging, important endeavor. In fact, it is incredibly important. Leaders bear tremendous responsibility for the present and future well-being of their communities and of human society in general. But you knew that already. The truth is, however, that followers are just as important—and bear just as much responsibility—as leaders. Following well is just as exciting and challenging, and requires just as much courage, as leading. And neither leading nor following requires formal authority or position. There is good reason to believe that anyone, from any position, can lead. The same is true of those following.

It all comes down to a choice: lead, follow, or get out of the way. There are important things to do. I hope this book helps you do them.

Joseph D. Potts, Contributing Editor
University of Kansas

PREFACE

John Gardner writes, "The first step is not action; the first step is understanding" (1990, *xiv*). Great people over the centuries have grappled with the meaning of effective leadership. In that same spirit of inquiry, our goal is to inform and stimulate rather than to "mold" future leaders. As with any subject, knowledge of the basics—those great thoughts that have shaped understanding about that subject—is the foundational platform upon which to build your knowledge of leadership.

From those early ideas, however, the concept of leadership is changing in exciting ways. Our own views of leadership diverge from more traditional, authority-centered approaches in favor of contemporary views emphasizing the common good, risk, collaboration, and civic responsibility. Newer theories in leadership are having an impact in executive suites, public institutions, and communities. We hope our students will carry the mantle of leadership throughout society, committed to making a difference in every kind of context.

This book was created because of our desire to help students understand the many dimensions of leadership theory. Our aim was to develop a readable workbook/textbook that would provide a comprehensive overview of the major theories in leadership studies. It is not intended, however, to be heavily theoretical. We include only the basic elements of the various conceptions of leadership. Our interest is in surveying ideas, their importance to leaders and followers, and their applicability to the process of leadership.

The academic study of leadership has boomed over the last decade. Our interest in the field came early in our academic careers. We are thankful that our university had the foresight to allow us to develop a strong academic leadership program that is accessible to any student. If we truly want to make a difference, it must be clear to all that leadership is not just for the few who have formal authority or a lot of money.

This text would be incomplete without a heartfelt thanks to a few key people. Leadership instructor Jill Stafford played an instrumental role in editing and putting this book together. In addition, Angie Flax, a student intern, also served as a writing editor. We would also like to thank our editor, Joe Potts, for extensively revising and improving this new edition, and for contributing Chapter 12. Finally, we would like to thank our many students at Fort Hays State University for their insightful questions, comments, and feedback. We are indebted to all of you.

C.B. Crawford
Curtis L. Brungardt
Micol Maughan

UNIT ONE

THE BASICS

Scholars have long struggled to formulate a basic definition of leadership. This unit introduces and discusses the most important definitions, and examines historical factors that have prompted frequent reconsiderations of the meaning of leadership

CHAPTER 1

DEFINING LEADERSHIP

Humans are intensely interested in differentiating leaders from non-leaders. In an academic sense, fields of study such as history, political science, and business management have arisen largely because of this innate human preoccupation. In recent decades, the implicit concern with leadership characterizing these diverse fields has spawned the development of more formal explicit programs of study focusing on the phenomenon of leadership itself. Whether the study of leadership has attained, or should attain, the status of an academic discipline in its own right is a point of some debate. It cannot be denied, however, that leadership is extremely important. But defining it is difficult. What distinguishes leaders from other people? And what is the difference between leadership and management? This chapter will introduce you to some of the complexities underlying those questions, and briefly review some of the better-known attempts to answer them.

CHAPTER OBJECTIVES

After studying this chapter you should be able to:
- √ recognize underlying problems in defining leadership,
- √ summarize the history of the terms "leader" and "leadership",
- √ explain various ways that leadership has been defined,
- √ explain some apparent differences between leadership and management, and
- √ list and explain common myths about leadership.

INTRODUCTION

What is leadership? Answers to this seemingly simple question are surprisingly diverse. Few questions generate debate as quickly as this one. But despite the difficulty of pinning down a definition, most people agree that leadership occurs around them with more or less frequency, and believe they can quickly point to examples of it. Understanding leadership behavior, as with any other human behavior, involves attempting to describe and interpret that behavior. When it comes to leadership, however, one person's interpretation is often another person's misinterpretation.

Although the word "leadership" only came into use relatively recently, it can be argued that the phenomenon it refers to has been occurring in human society for a very long time. Many terms might be associated more or less closely with leadership. Consider the following list:

- presidency
- authority
- command
- responsibility
- control
- influence
- management
- supervision
- dictatorship

- guide
- rule
- administration
- direction
- boss
- government
- executive
- master
- coordination

Any description of leadership begins with one or more assumptions, whether or not they are clearly stated.

In any given situation, the terms used to identify or describe leadership suggest certain underlying assumptions. For example, it might be assumed that leadership has to do with certain types of *actions*, or, on the other hand, that it is associated with certain *positions* in an organization or society. Some descriptions suggest that leadership has certain *effects*. That is, leaders are identified as people who cause other people to behave in certain ways, or cause certain things to happen. It might also be assumed that leadership has to do with the *relationship* between one category of persons (leaders) and another (followers). Any description or definition of leadership begins with one or more assumptions such as these, whether or not those assumptions are clearly stated.

Are some of these assumptions right and others wrong? How can we know? Assumptions of any kind tend to make us nervous. Saying we "assume" something can feel like an admission that we lack evidence in support of our position. This need not be the case, however. Logicians tell us that to describe anything, we must make assumptions. We must assume certain things about leadership in order to describe it, but we should choose our assumptions responsibly. That is, we should be able to point to logic and evidence that support our view.

But if leadership is so difficult to understand, and open to so many different interpretations, why attempt to study it? The authors of this book offer one uncomplicated answer to that question. Leadership is worthy of study because it has such a direct, and often profound, impact on individuals and societies (and here we present our most basic assumption: our belief that leadership has important effects). Leadership should be studied because of what leadership does. The fact that leadership is so difficult to understand only provides further justification for our argument that leadership should be studied formally. Leadership can be improved—its effects can be made more beneficial—if its nature and processes are better understood.

Over the past century, a number of very capable scholars have attempted to define leadership and explain how it works. Elaborate models and theories have been developed. This book is essentially a broad survey of the most significant ideas and theories about leadership. What is leadership? The diversity of answers you encounter herein should convince you that the question cannot be taken lightly.

A BRIEF HISTORICAL OVERVIEW

James MacGregor Burns summed up the state of affairs regarding leadership when he described it as "one of the most observed, but least understood" of all human behaviors. Nineteenth and early twentieth century definitions of leadership were in fact descriptions of what "leaders" *did*, and assumed that the actions, traits, feelings, or attitudes being described were "leadership." Over time it became obvious that simply describing or analyzing the behaviors of certain individuals begged the more fundamental question. Why had those individuals been identified as "leaders" in the first place? It had been assumed that leaders were persons in certain types of positions, but that assumption was flawed. People often led despite not being in a particular type of formal position, and many actions of persons in formal positions of power or authority obviously had nothing to do with leadership. Leadership would have to be defined in terms that had nothing to do with position.

One could easily assume that the idea or concept of leadership has been around for thousands of years, but in fact it seems to have been specifically labeled as such only relatively recently. In English, the appearance of the word "leadership" can be traced to about 200 years ago. The term "leader," however, has been around since approximately 1300 A.D. Rost (1990) suggests that modern English "to lead" has its roots in the Old English "leden," which meant "to make go" or "to guide." The term "leadership" first appeared in an English dictionary in 1828 when Webster defined it as "the condition of being a leader." That definition assumed, as discussed above, that leadership was what leaders did, and that who leaders were was self-evident. The definition was circular, in effect saying very little. Importantly, however, it did give a name to a phenomenon that previously had none.

> *Early definitions assumed that leadership was simply what leaders did, and that who the "leaders" were was self-evident.*

Since the mid-1900's, leadership has been defined numerous ways. Many of these definitions are the product of particular theories about leadership. Bass (1990) summarized these theories as falling into the following distinct categories:

- leadership as group process
- leadership as personality
- leadership as the gaining of compliance
- leadership as influence
- leadership as action or behavior
- leadership as persuasion
- leadership as a power relation
- leadership as an instrument of goal attainment
- leadership as product of interaction
- leadership as a differentiated role
- leadership as the initiation of structure

All told, Bass catalogued more than 100 different ways of defining leadership. In each of Bass's categories, one or more definitions of leadership can be found expressing that particular theoretical orientation. Since 1990, several more categories can be added to Bass's list.

- leadership as the facilitation of change
- leadership as organizational improvement
- leadership as the confronting (challenging) of authority
- leadership as ethics

LEADERSHIP VS. MANAGEMENT

How is leadership to be distinguished from management? Mintzberg (1973) contended that leadership was merely a form or subset of management, one of a number of functions required of managers. In addition to "leader," Mintzberg's list contained the following managerial roles or functions:

- figurehead
- negotiator
- liaison
- monitor
- disseminator

- spokesman
- entrepreneur
- disturbance handler
- resource allocator

Many scholars dispute the view that anyone who can manage can also lead.

Other scholars have strongly objected to views like Mintzberg's, disputing in particular the implication that anyone who can manage can also lead. Noted leadership theorists such as Warren Bennis & Bert Nanus (1985), John Gardner (1990), Kotter (1990), and Joseph Rost (1991) argue instead that leadership and management have very little in common. As Bennis and Nanus put it,

> [T]here is a profound difference between management and leadership, and both are important. 'To manage' means 'to bring about, to accomplish, to have charge of or responsibility for, to conduct.' Leading is 'influencing, guiding in direction, course, action, opinion.' The distinction is crucial. Managers are people who do things right and leaders are people who do the right thing. The difference may be summarized as activities of vision and judgment; effectiveness versus activities of mastering routines [or] efficiency (p. 21).

Kotter carefully analyzes and categorizes differences he sees between leadership and management. These differences are outlined on the following page.

Many other scholars have written on the distinction between leadership and management, and much more could be said on the topic. For now, however, it is sufficient to note that many contemporary theorists believe that the two concepts, though related, differ in fundamental ways.

Kotter's Leadership Taxonomy

Action Criteria	Leadership	Management
Agenda Building	- establishes direction - develops a vision - develops strategies for achievement	- plans and budgets - establishes steps and timelines for results - allocates resources
Networking	- aligns people - communicates direction - creates teams and coalitions and accepts their conclusions - fosters and grows the vision	- organizes and staffs - establishes structures and benchmarks - delegates elements of projects - develops policy - monitors relationships
Execution	- motivates and inspires - energizes people to achieve - meets human needs - finds ways to overcome barriers	- controls and solves problems - monitors results - fixes problems
Outcomes	- productive, useful, innovative change - motivation and inspiration	- stability, efficiency, bureaucracy - predictability and order - consistent results for stakeholders

MYTHS OF LEADERSHIP

Scholarly analyses of leadership tell part of the story, but the ideas of non-scholars reveal important assumptions and beliefs about leadership that are extremely helpful in an introduction to the topic. Brungardt (1995) surveyed college undergraduates and found commonly held ideas that were unsupported by the literature. He referred to these false assumptions as the "great myths of leadership." Brungardt's research suggested that many college undergraduates see leadership as directive, controlling, and functional. His research identified ten commonly held myths, briefly summarized below as a final preface to the formal theories of leadership presented in subsequent chapters.

Myth 1 - Leaders are born, not made

This idea calls to mind references in common vernacular to "born leaders," but a substantial amount of writing in the leadership literature of recent decades focuses on disproving the notion that some individuals are born with endowed qualities that make them the only ones who can truly lead. Research now suggests that leadership abilities are generally learned and often contextual. Individuals can of course be born with genetic characteristics that predispose them to be more or less extroverted, organized, or intelligent. In and of themselves, however, no single attributes or combination of attributes is a formula for natural leadership ability.

Myth 2 - Leaders lead, followers follow

It seems logical to simply assume that leaders lead and followers follow, but in fact leadership is often shared, distributed, or contextual. An individual can lead, for example, in the context of a meeting, then walk out of the meeting onto the factory floor and assume the role of follower. Is that individual a leader or a follower? The answer is both. This simple observation makes a critical point: leaders and followers are not discrete, non-overlapping groups. The fact that the same person can be both leader and follower is an important clue to the nature of leadership.

Myth 3 - Leadership is basically good management

A large body of scholarly work in recent years has argued persuasively, if not conclusively, that management is qualitatively different from leadership. Many writers are convinced that leading others involves at minimum a "big picture" process that involves sharing power, focusing on a particular vision, and empowering others to achieve great things. For managers, details seem to dominate, making their focus primarily the nuts and bolts of daily operation.

Myth 4 - Charisma is necessary for leadership

Effective leadership is commonly associated with charismatic personalities, but research has shown that dynamic, colorful leaders are rarely essential in achieving a vision. Charisma can be an important attribute of leadership, but it is neither a sufficient nor necessary condition for effectiveness. Many capable leaders cannot be described as particularly dynamic, colorful, or inspiring. Neither Dwight Eisenhower nor Bill Gates can be described as charismatic, but both effectively lead others to achieve great things.

Myth 5 - Leadership is power

Leadership is often assumed to depend upon the ability to wield power, but whereas power tends to limit the options of others, studies show that leadership attempts to create options. Strategies and processes based on power preclude sharing it, for sharing reduces the primary means of influence. Leadership processes, on the other hand, distribute power as only one of several means of change. Much in the contemporary leadership literature suggests that leadership involves a self-limiting, self-constraining dimension based on the moral principle of respect for individual autonomy. Raw power-wielding makes no place for principles limiting the ways power can be used.

Myth 6 - Leadership is position

John Gardner's (1990) work explicitly addressed this idea, arguing instead that leadership is a relationship. Gardner and other theorists make a strong case that management is best understood as a position, whereas leadership is a process that takes place through the medium of relationships. Leadership can therefore occur in the context of a group whose members cannot be distinguished from one another on the basis of any formal difference in rank or position.

Myth 7 - Leaders do anything to stay on top

College students surveyed during Brungardt's research frequently suggested that leaders are simply individuals who are willing to do whatever it takes to remain in positions of authority. This view is a combination of the two previous myths regarding leadership as power and position. Interestingly, a growing body of work suggests that genuine leaders are willing to sacrifice power, position or both if necessary to avoid violating principles more important than the simple attainment of particular goals.

Leadership now seems to be defined more by *how* goals are pursued than it is by whether or not those goals are achieved.

Myth 8 - Leaders control events, events don't control leaders

A number of students surveyed identified leaders as those individuals who seemed to possess the ability to control what took place around them. Like the preceding idea, however, this view is problematic given that leadership is often identified in situations that do not involve the successful achievement of specified goals. Leadership often develops or occurs precisely when responses are needed to events beyond any person's control.

Myth 9 - Leaders tell people what to do, followers do it

The concept here sounds similar to the second myth above, but in fact expresses a very different belief by going a step further in assuming that leaders are a separate group who tell other people (followers) what to do. The literature now shows, however, that leaders tend to empower others rather than control them. Leadership also tends to employ means of influence that result in positive relationships, whereas simply exerting power or imposing will on others does not result in positive relationships.

Myth 10 - Leadership is what leaders do

As discussed earlier, this common misconception is the product of circular thinking. Describing or defining leadership as something "leaders" do simply begs the question. How are the "leaders" identified? What activities, positions or characteristics were used to identify them as such? Most scholars now agree that leadership has to do with relationships in that it is something leaders and followers engage in together.

SUMMARY

John Gardner, in his 1990 book *On Leadership*, captured the importance of thinking about concepts and definitions when he asserted that "the first step is not action; the first step is understanding" (p. xiv). Leadership is a complex phenomenon that is easily (and commonly) misunderstood. It does not necessarily relate to formal positions, it does not involve wielding power, it is not defined by the achievement of specified goals, and it seems to have very little in common with management. What is leadership? Having identified some common myths about leadership, the chapters that follow offer a number of potential answers.

REFERENCES

Bass, B. M. (1990). *Bass and Stogdill's handbook of leadership: Theory, research, and managerial application.* (3rd edition). New York: Free Press.

Bennis, W. & Nanus, B. (1985). *Leaders: The strategies for taking charge.* New York: Harper & Row.

Brungardt, C. L. (1995). Great myths of leadership. Unpublished paper.

Burns, J. M. (1978). *Leadership.* New York: Free Press.

Gardner, J. W (1990). *On leadership.* New York: Free Press.

Kotter, J. P. (1990). *A force for change: How leadership differs from management.* New York: Free Press.

Mintzberg, H. (1973). *The nature of managerial work.* New York: Harper & Row.

Rost, J. C. (1991). *Leadership for the twenty-first century.* Westport, CT: Preager.

Chapter 1   Name _____

DISCUSSION QUESTIONS

1. What are the organizational implications of assuming that leaders are born and not made?

_____

_____

_____

_____

_____

_____

_____

_____

_____

2. At this point in your thinking, how would you explain the difference between leaders and managers?

_____

_____

_____

_____

_____

_____

_____

_____

_____

3. How would you respond to someone who asserted that "leadership is what leaders do"?

_____

_____

_____

_____

_____

_____

_____

_____

_____

_____

_____

_____

_____

_____

_____

_____

_____

_____

3. How would you respond to someone who asserted that "leadership is what leaders do"?

Name _____

CASE STUDY

Leadership is embodied in the relationship between the leader and the follower. In the following case study, try to imagine what the people involved are thinking. Also, identify the behaviors that are occurring. Then develop your answers to the questions that follow.

The Case of Dundee Consulting Inc.

It was Friday, April 16 and the final mailing was being hand delivered to the U. S. Post Office. Max Forest was in charge of the Southern Rockies Tax Accounting division of Dundee Consulting. Max's group was comprised of twelve accountants, an office manager, and four office staff members. Max and his team had worked nearly 16-hour days for the last month to complete the stacks of tax documents for the hundred or so clients they served in the tri-state area. Max had personally put in nearly 100 hours in the last week and was as physically and emotionally exhausted as everyone else on the accounting team. About half of the team asked to take part of the next week off in order to recover from the heavy schedule they had kept over the last quarter. The rest of the group would be in the office, but Max knew they were finalizing important loose ends with late filings. The tax season was even more tense because Max had been told in January that his division might be closed if revenue from the tax season was not substantial enough to justify the huge payroll and high overhead cost of the plush office in downtown Denver.

Max had just received an email from Dundee Vice President of Domestic Operations, Jimmie Walls. Jimmie announced that he was going to be in the Denver area on Monday, April 19 and would like to meet with Max and his team to assess earnings of the division during the recently ended first quarter. Jimmie proposed that the team and Max compile and analyze as much income data as they could by Monday and present that information over a luncheon meeting. Max realized that the amount of time needed just to collect the data would be well over 20 hours, even for the most veteran team associates. Max also realized that a poor showing (in either the data or the presentation) would greatly impact, perhaps fatally, the future of the Southern Rockies division. The meeting had to be held, it had to be flawless, and the data had to be presented effectively if the team (and possibly even Max) were to have any hope of being retained by Dundee.

Considering these factors, please answer the questions on the following page.

1. If Max were to engage in *leadership,* what actions would he take? Discuss each basic element needed to deliver the best possible meeting on Monday.

_____

_____

_____

_____

_____

_____

_____

_____

_____

2. If Max were to engage in *management,* what actions would he take to insure the best possible outcome on Monday?

_____

_____

_____

_____

_____

_____

_____

_____

_____

CHAPTER 2

THE HISTORY OF LEADERSHIP

The development of leadership is a fascinating, critical thread in the unfolding of human history and the advancement of civilization. From the dawn of civilization to modern post-industrial society, leaders have exerted enormous influence on the development of the human race.

CHAPTER OBJECTIVES

After studying this chapter you should be able to:

√ understand the importance of the history of leadership,

√ identify qualities of tribal leadership,

√ understand pre-classical leadership,

√ identify classical leadership,

√ identify progressive leadership,

√ understand post-progressive leadership,

√ compare each leadership era,

√ synthesize the leadership eras, and

√ trace the progression of leadership development.

INTRODUCTION

Everything has a history. Understanding the historical underpinnings of leadership will help us better understand why we are where we are today. Leadership, like many other forms of human interaction, is difficult to trace to its particular origin. As Bass writes, "The study of leadership rivals in age the emergence of civilization, which shaped its leaders as much as it was shaped by them." Like the institutions of marriage or religion, the exact date when leadership took shape would be impossible to determine. But there is still good reason to believe that leadership occurred early in the course of human history.

TRIBAL LEADERSHIP

> *"The study of leadership has been the study of leaders - what they did and why they did it."*
>
> *Bernard Bass*

It's not hard to imagine that early human organizations, tribes and families, developed leadership to some extent. In tribal communities, leaders probably assumed the role of coordinators and skilled experts. The leadership relationship was probably more directive and task-oriented than personal or social. Tribal leaders were probably "elected" based more on their size, strength, and agility than on their good looks or interpersonal skills. Tribal leaders were most likely skilled hunters, which gave them the right to lead, in contrast to the qualifications for leadership in later, more complex social structures. Leadership was probably based more on strong survival skills, and a perceived ability to manage fear of the unknown, than on charisma, personality traits, or behaviors.

In early tribal communities, family leadership was perhaps the most important form of leadership. The limited development of social structures meant that family relationships were as important as hunting and gathering relationships. Familial relationships represented the primary source of training in social and survival skills, and were the only potentially stable source of security and support for individuals. In family units, leadership was probably more collaborative and person-centered and less hierarchical than in the hunting party.

PRE-CLASSICAL LEADERSHIP

As we turn the clock forward to pre-modern times, ranging roughly from early Old Testament times to the beginning of the Enlightenment, important elements of leadership changed significantly. Cultures throughout this very long period were particularly concerned with spirituality. The same sort of ability to manage fear was called for, just as in pre-civilized times, but there were new things to fear as well. Death was feared, but the afterlife was a bigger mystery and feared even more. Leadership theorist Gilbert Fairholm notes that, prior to modernity, the great people in society were not just the strongest, the smartest, or those who controlled resources. Chiefs, priests, and kings also served as a window or channel to larger reality. "They claimed to have the ear of the gods, receiving inspiration and visions from above." It was their responsibility, their necessary role, to give sense to life. Some sort of access to or understanding of magic and the spiritual world were important qualifications that separated the leaders from non-leaders.

As spirituality became a critical element in leadership, the development of nobility and royalty formalized leadership relative to particular regions or territories. Despite the important role of various kinds of assistants (generals, warriors, knights, scribes), the authority of kings in creating policy for their "kingdoms" was unquestioned. This melding of spiritual and administrative authority came to be known as "divine right," and served to justify the wielding of power by monarchs for thousands of years, even into some cultures in the modern world. Kings were understood to draw their power from the gods, and were obliged to rule with benevolence. Upon their death, kings in some societies were lavishly entombed and given the spiritual status of gods.

One of the most important writers relative to leadership theory in pre-modernity was Nicollo Machiavelli. Machiavelli's best-known writings recommended strategies for kings and princes to use so as to more effectively wield power and manipulate subjects. Today the work of Machiavelli and others advocating similar views are often viewed with disgust. But Machiavelli's work was rather liberal in pre-modernity, because he acknowledged the importance of skills beyond the simple use of brute force to govern a kingdom. Pre-classical theory is still evident today in countries where democracy has yet to be embraced.

CLASSICAL LEADERSHIP

Classical leadership can generally be linked to changes in government and society that have taken place since the Enlightenment. However, the primary assumption of classical leadership—maximal production at minimal cost—has been influential since pre-modernity. The purposes of many leaders in the classical mold can be boiled down to one rudimentary objective: the creation of stable profit. Stability is key in the classical organization. Change is often seen as disruptive to workflow and a source of increased error and decreased predictably in the business or government equation. Classical leadership is measured not by body counts, but by the number of rifles produced, bricks laid, or bushels of cotton picked.

Classical leadership assumes that leaders have the authority to make decisions, confront issues, make others accountable, as well as—in a business context—hire and evaluate employees. Classical leaders further assume that they have a duty, or right, to perform leadership in the way they see best. This form of leadership limits the contribution of followers to following directions. Classical leaders generally share a belief that workers are naturally inefficient, and if left to their own devices, could not perform at a satisfactory level. Leaders in this tradition generally use directive, and sometimes coercive, means to get the job done. Classical leaders do what it takes to get the job done in the most expedient and efficient manner possible.

> *Classical leaders generally share the belief that workers are inefficient, and if left to their own devices, will not perform at a satisfactory level.*

One implication arising from classical theory is that not everyone can lead. Only those persons in formal leadership positions are leaders. That is, positions justify the actions of leaders.

Classical leaders organize, control, command, decide, and manipulate so as to optimize results. The most effective leaders in this vein are those who can impose structure in chaotic situations. The capacity to organize is absolutely essential for the classical leader. Given the fact that the classicist desires stability and to minimize change, formal structure is the best means of codifying what is good in the organization. In large organizations, formal policies implement and enforce the classical leader's directives. These formalized policies, detailed in corporate manuals and employee handbooks, for example, serve to keep leaders in power and keep workers working. Policies are designed to stabilize, organize and make more efficient the naturally inefficient workers in potentially chaotic organizations. They reinforce the status quo and minimize change.

PROGRESSIVE LEADERSHIP

In terms of business leadership, it became apparent to most of corporate America by the mid-1970s that *stability* was no longer the best prescription for organizational health. Relatively easy growth that had characterized the 1950s, 1960s, and much of the 1970s was no longer happening. Economic conditions had become much more competitive and volatile due to a combination of increased global competition, regulatory demands, new micro-economic trends, technological changes, and demographic shifts in the workplace. Classical leadership and the slow, incremental organizational change and improvement it valued would no longer be adequate.

Business leaders began to realize that they would have to increase quality and reduce costs to insure growth, to compete, and to survive in this new environment. Corporate leaders began playing a new game – the *change* game. The 1980s and 1990s witnessed an explosion of new management techniques and approaches designed to enhance organizational growth. The quality movement (TQM and CQI, for example), re-engineering, strategic thinking and planning, change management, and organizational improvement all represented attempts to implement major corporate change. The watchword was change—companies realized that if they did not change, they would die.

The challenge facing business leaders was to promote, encourage, and master the art of organizational change. In this new business climate, top management began to serve as a *change agent* in the hope of transforming their organizations. Their responsibility was now to provide the foresight and energy necessary to carry change forward. Progressive leadership called for leaders to move out of traditional roles and begin to lead organizations through the sometimes painful process of real change. As change agents, leaders created the vision and direction for the group. In addition to providing this direction, they initiated the change process. Progressive leaders saw themselves as being responsible for directing the structure, processes, and culture of their organizations through the change process.

As the overall purpose of business leadership changed from status quo thinking to organizational change, so too did the methods used by business leaders to effect that change. Employees at all levels increasingly expressed the desire for empowerment, for more decision-making power and responsibility in their work environment. Experts also began to point to the increasing availability of information as an additional reason to move away from hierarchical structures.

Employees at all levels want to feel empowered and have more decision-making responsibility.

Business literature today describes a management style or approach radically different from the traditional idea of leadership in which the leader is tough-minded, in control, and operating from the top of a hierarchy. It is now recognized that business leaders need to play the role of collaborators and facilitators. Many different models or approaches to empowerment have been developed, but all revolve around the simple concept of shared power. All of these models call for top management to transfer power to lower levels of the organization so as to "maximize the full potential" of all employees.

Eras of Leadership

Age of Leadership	Implications for Leaders	Implications for Followers
Tribal	- Brute force accepted, fear-based - Survival skills rule - Coordinator, skilled expert	- Failure to follow leads to death - Follower's role important for tribal success - Long-term power derived from survival skills
Pre-Classical	- Spiritual or magical elements - Male dominant - Divine right - Brutality and oppression justified	- Subservient role - Vessels to be filled with spiritual teachings or law - Subhuman treatment accepted - Follow because of or through fear
Classical	- Production at all costs - Labor is infinite - Leaders lead and divide labor - Organize, control, command, decide, and manipulate for results	- Hard work expected, and "builds character" - Chaos is the enemy of the policy-driven organization - No one indispensable - Workers naturally lazy and inefficient
Progressive	- Stability no longer the key - Change game, TQM, and re-engineering - Change agent, visionary for transformational change - Empowerment the mantra, "Unlock the potential of everyone"	- Everyone has worth and value - Collaboration means more power for followers, shared power - Intimate involvement with total organizational change - Needs met on management's terms - Organization's needs met
Post-Progressive	- Answers to issues in the post-industrial world - New democratic agenda - Social change, ethics, collaboration, and risk leadership models	- Collaboration and agenda building are the new roles of the follower - Equal partner in the leadership relationship - Followers' needs met - Society's needs met

Modern approaches seek to create organizations that are flat and flexible as possible, and emphasize informal networks for collaboration and communication, decentralized accountability, and shared power. Sharing power across the organization is seen as a strategy for "unlocking the potential" of all employees.

POST-PROGRESSIVE LEADERSHIP

Leaders today must be sensitive to the demands of the information society and the expectations of a post Cold War world. Accordingly, new forms of leadership have emerged that seek to explore the world of leadership beyond business. Post-progressive theories of leadership will be discussed in later chapters. These propose to change the basic fabric of the leadership relationship in all areas of society. Social change models, risk leadership, and leadership as ethics all represent efforts to define truly progressive models for leader-follower relations in the context of modern life.

SUMMARY

In leadership, as in any other field, an understanding of history is important in order so as to avoid remaking mistakes already made at some point in the past. We can avoid experiencing again atrocities such as those of World War II if we study and understand the leadership failures that contributed to those atrocities. Every conception of leadership brings with it certain strengths and weaknesses. As we face another era of leadership development, we must keep one eye on the past and the other on the current and anticipated needs and realities of world society.

REFERENCES

Bass, B. M. (1990). *Bass and Stogdill's handbook of leadership: Theory, research, and managerial application.* (3rd edition). New York: Free Press.

DuBrin, A. J. (1998*). Leadership: Research, findings, practice, and skills.* (2nd ed.). Boston, MA: Houghton-Mifflin.

Fairholm, G. (1991). *Values leadership: Toward a New Philosophy of Leadership.* New York: Praeger.

Gardner, J.W. (1990). *On leadership.* New York: The Free Press.

Hornstein, H. A. (1996). *Brutal bosses and their prey.* New York: Riverhead.

Northouse, P.G. (2001). *Leadership: Theory and practice.* (2nd ed.). Thousand Oaks, CA: Sage Publications.

Wren, J. T. (1995). *The leader's companion: Insights on leadership through the ages.* New York: Free Press.

Yukl, G. A. (1989). *Leadership in organizations.* (2nd edition). Englewood Cliffs, NJ: Prentice-Hall.

Yukl, G.A. (2003). *Leadership in organizations.* (5th edition), Upper Saddle River, NJ: Prentice-Hall.

Chapter 2   **Name** _____

DISCUSSION QUESTIONS

1. Imagine yourself as a leader in a past era. Name the era and describe how you would handle a specific problem or situation.

   _____

   _____

   _____

   _____

   _____

   _____

   _____

   _____

   _____

2. Talk to someone who was in the workforce in the 1960's, and ask them what leadership was like in that classical era. Report what you find out, and then tell what changes you think have taken place in leadership since then.

   _____

   _____

   _____

   _____

   _____

   _____

   _____

   _____

   _____

   _____

3. Imagine yourself in a leadership situation. What behaviors and skills, in your best estimate, will be necessary to successfully lead others?

_____

_____

_____

_____

_____

_____

_____

_____

_____

_____

_____

_____

_____

_____

_____

_____

_____

_____

Chapter 2   **Name** _____

ACTIVITY

Consider each of the following situations and compare the actions of leaders from at least three different eras. Write what you think they would do in **each** of the situations in the space provided.

1. You are on a mountainside, miles away from any settlement. A member of your climbing party has been severely hurt and cannot continue. You are the designated decision-maker for the group. What do you do?

Tribal approach: _____

_____

_____

_____

_____

Classical approach: _____

_____

_____

_____

_____

_____

Post-progressive approach: _____

_____

_____

_____

_____

_____

2. You are preparing to lead a group of soldiers into a potentially fatal battle. As the battalion commander, you are looked to for leadership. What approach will you use to increase the likelihood of victory?

Pre-classical approach: _____

_____

_____

_____

_____

_____

Classical approach:_____

_____

_____

_____

_____

_____

_____

Progressive approach: _____

_____

_____

_____

_____

_____

UNIT TWO

THEORIES OF LEADERSHIP

An understanding of the larger history of leadership is essential, but the preponderance of writing about leadership has been produced relatively recently, over the past 100 years. Trait theory, behavioral theory, situational and contingency theory, power and influence theory, and transformational theory have all been proposed as answers to questions of leadership. This unit discusses each of these major areas of leadership theory.

CHAPTER 3

TRAIT THEORIES

This chapter discusses the first formal theory of leadership—trait theory. This approach to leadership focuses on the personal traits and characteristics of leaders. Both traditional and contemporary research in leadership traits and skills are reviewed.

CHAPTER OBJECTIVES

After studying this chapter you should be able to:

√ understand the implications of the nature vs. nurture question,

√ recognize the important role trait research plays in the study of leadership,

√ identify the key elements and variables of Stogdill's research,

√ understand the strengths and weaknesses of the trait approach to leadership,

√ understand the basic components of charismatic leadership, and

√ understand the elements of contemporary trait theories.

INTRODUCTION

Researchers and social scientists of the early twentieth century believed that leaders possessed certain traits that enabled them to lead others. These unique physical and psychological characteristics provided them with the ability and potential to influence others. At the time, most scholars assumed that these traits were personal characteristics that were inherited. Later, this view was expanded to include skills learned and developed through life experiences. These earlier leadership researchers were not sure which traits were the most essential; however, they did believe that a person's physical and psychological characteristics were the best gauge for leadership potential. Most of these traits fell into the following categories: physical characteristics, social background, intelligence and ability, personality, task related abilities, and social characteristics (Bass, 1990).

NATURE VS. NURTURE

One of the most important questions that trait theorists attempted to answer had to do with the origin of leadership traits. Many trait theorists believed that people were born with skills that made them leaders. If they were born into "good stock" or had families with wealth and/or intellect, they were automatically leaders. These born leaders (Rockefellers, DuPonts, and others) were held in the highest esteem during that time. Other trait theorists contended that traits had to do less with the characteristics one was born with, and more with the environment in which one grew up. These theorists pointed to leaders like Horatio Alger and Dale Carnegie in the industrial world. This debate raged for years and much research attempted to prove or disprove one position or the other.

Most people considering the issue today believe that leadership ability is influenced by one's birthright, but leadership can also be learned.

Over the years, the nature versus nurture debate has become less important. As research continued, it became clear that the answer was not nearly as simple as either side wanted it to be. Most theorists today begin with the assumption that an individual's repertoire of leadership abilities is impacted by his or her birthright, but leadership is also learnable. The truth seems to be that both nature and nurture play a role in the development of personality traits. The traits of leaders are not due exclusively either to nature or to one's environment and experiences.

EARLIEST THEORIES

The *great man theory* is considered to be one of the earliest theories of leadership. Popular among researchers of the late nineteenth and early twentieth century, this theory argued that those who served as leaders were "endowed" differently from others. It was believed that leaders were more capable and had certain traits that the rest of society did not possess. The great leaders of history like George Washington, Winston Churchill, and Martin Luther King, to mention just a few, possessed qualities that their fellow countrymen did not. These leaders were believed to be "great men" who provided direction and influenced the masses.

Social scientists of the early twentieth century believed that leaders possessed certain traits that enabled them to lead others.

The great man theory led to considerable research, but the conclusion reached by many scholars of the time was that leaders were in fact not that different from others. The diversity of leaders seemed to indicate to researchers that very different sorts of people had been successful at leading others. As a result, the great man theory slowly faded away as a serious field of study by the early 1900s. This failure encouraged the development and evolution of the trait theory approach. Rather than searching for "great men," researchers began looking for the personal traits that enabled leaders to lead. The idea was that, if leaders did possess unique qualities and characteristics, it must then be possible to identify these leader traits. During this time period, trait theory produced a considerable amount of empirical research that provided scholars with insight into leaders and their personal traits.

STOGDILL'S 1948 REVIEW

Ralph Stogdill published a comprehensive review in 1948 that compiled nearly 130 leader trait studies from 1904 to 1947. Stogdill's review identified six common variables from these studies that included personal characteristics as well as situational factors. The six variables were:

- *Capacity.* This includes personal traits, such as intelligence, communication skills, and judgement. These critical elements directly affect a leader's capacity to lead. Leaders are believed to be more intelligent than others and to have the ability to communicate ideas clearly.

- *Achievement.* Those who have achieved a great deal in their lives are more likely to be elevated to leadership roles. Personal achievements, such as a college degree or certificate in a particular field, are seen as factors that provide the individual with the necessary abilities to lead.

- *Responsibility.* Stogdill's research showed that, generally speaking, those who choose to lead are responsible to themselves, their followers, and to their cause or organization. Leaders are also seen as dependable and are persistent in pursuing their goals.

- *Participation.* Leaders are not spectators, but rather are active players in the groups and organizations in which they belong. Simply, leaders are willing to get involved, to participate, and to contribute in activities of the larger group.

- *Status.* The studies also suggested that a person's socioeconomic status and position directly relate to leadership and leadership potential. Generally, those who held leadership positions came from higher or more prosperous socioeconomic backgrounds and from more prestigious families.

- *Situation.* Although not a personal trait, Stogdill's research showed that situational factors play a large part in leadership, leadership effectiveness, and in determining which individuals serve as leaders. The studies indicated that being a leader in one situation did not guarantee action as a leader in another.

Despite the enormous amount of research on personal traits reviewed by Stogdill, few if any traits were found to be universally essential to the leadership process. Instead, he found that the need for certain traits varied based on the situation. In addition, he found many successful leaders who did not exhibit common traits. These early studies did not produce a particular "set of traits" that alone would guarantee leadership (Bass, 1990).

STOGDILL'S 1974 REVIEW

In 1974, Stogdill again conducted an extensive review of the research in trait theory. This time, he reviewed and analyzed more than 160 independent trait studies published between 1949 and 1970. His conclusions incorporated information from his 1948 review as well. Stogdill suggested the following trait profile:

> *The leader is characterized by a strong drive for responsibility and task completion, persistence in pursuit of goals, venture in problem solving, drive to exercise initiative in social situations, self-confidence and sense of personal identity, willingness to accept consequences of decision and action, readiness to absorb interpersonal stress, willingness to tolerate frustration and delay, ability to influence other persons' behavior, and capacity to structure social interaction systems to the purpose at hand.*

Below is a list of the personal traits and skills Stogdill found to be common among successful leaders:

- adaptable
- achievement-oriented
- assertive
- cooperative
- decisive
- dependable
- dominant
- energetic
- persistent
- willing to assume responsibility

- intelligent
- creative
- diplomatic
- effective communication
- knowledge of tasks
- organized
- persuasive
- socially skilled
- self-confident
- tolerates stress

Although scholars before him had rejected many elements of trait theory, Stogdill continued to believe that by studying individual characteristics, a great deal could be learned about leadership. While most agree that trait research did not produce a "set of traits" that were absolutely necessary for leadership, it did provide a good understanding of common characteristics of those who serve as leaders. Today, most scholars believe that certain personal traits may enhance a person's ability to lead, but these characteristics by themselves do not guarantee leadership effectiveness.

CHARISMATIC THEORIES

Some of the more recent work in the field of trait theory has been in the study of personal charisma. Some researchers are looking at the relationship between those who are seen as charismatic people and how that might enhance their ability to lead. Historically, the Greek word charisma means "divinely inspired gift". Today, however, charisma is viewed more as a personality trait (or traits) that attract the attention of others.

In 1977, Robert House proposed a new theory based on the characteristics of charismatic leaders. House argued that charismatic leaders have a strong desire for power, are highly confident, and have a strong conviction about their own personal beliefs and ideals. This theory also states that charisma came first and foremost from followers' perceptions that the leader possesses unique qualities and characteristics.

House's Charismatic Theory includes:

- Charismatic leaders engage in behaviors that impress followers.
- Charismatic leaders communicate goals that are deeply shared among the followers.
- Charismatic leaders use emotional appeals to motivate followers.
- Charismatic leaders have high expectations of their followers.
- Charismatic leaders serve as role models for their followers.

In a more recent study, Conger and Kanungo (1998) proposed a charismatic leadership theory that was based primarily on followers' observations of leaders' behaviors. They believe that some followers attribute certain charismatic qualities and traits to a leader because of his or her behavior. These behaviors include:

- *Extreme vision*. Charismatic leaders often express a vision that is radically different from the status quo.
- *High personal risk*. Charismatic leaders often take great personal risks and make significant sacrifices to achieve their vision.
- *Use of unconventional strategies*. Charismatic leaders often achieve their goals through unconventional methods.
- *Communicate self-confidence*. Charismatic leaders express to their followers a high degree of confidence in themselves and the group's mission.

CONTEMPORARY TRAIT APPROACHES

Even though the effectiveness of trait approaches has been seriously questioned in both academic and practical contexts, many still believe some personal traits are predictive of leadership.

Covey's Habits and Principles

Stephen Covey identifies traits of leaders based on his assumption that people will be more effective at leading others if they are effective at leading their own lives. Covey (1991) defined "principle-centered leaders" as persons who:

- are continually learning
- see life as an adventure
- exercise for self-renewal
- believe in other people
- are service-oriented
- lead balanced lives
- are synergistic
- radiate positive energy

Covey's books have been widely embraced in recent popular literature. His devotees hold his "seven habits of highly effective people" in high regard. His list of habits should be recognized as a reiteration of trait theory. Those habits are:

1. Be proactive
2. Begin with the end in mind
3. Put first things first
4. Think win/win
5. Seek first to understand, then to be understood
6. Synergize
7. Sharpen the saw

The strength of Covey's approach, while non-empirical and anecdotal, is logical and compelling, as is evidenced by the number of adherents he has attracted. The seven habits (traits) seem rational, reasonable, and accessible to many who seek to improve their abilities as leaders.

Emotional Intelligence (EQ)

Recent work by Daniel Goleman (1998a, 1998b) and others into the idea of emotional intelligence illustrate the fact that trait research is still viable in the field of leadership. Goleman (1998a) concludes that leaders who are highly emotionally intelligent are:

- self-aware
- self-regulating
- motivated
- empathetic
- socially skilled

Goleman admits that intelligence and technical skills are important, but asserts that emotional intelligence differentiates the mediocre leader from the exceptional.

Based on Goleman's foundation, Cooper (1997) asserts that there are three essential driving forces within successful leaders. These driving forces are the key to the ability of leaders to have an impact on their followers and organizations. First, effective leaders build trusting relationships. This enables them to develop in a similar manner the capacity and character of their organization. Second, leaders work to increase the energy and effectiveness of organizations. This also develops capacity and stimulates initiative. Finally, emotionally intelligent leaders strive to shape the future by tapping the power of divergent views and making the most of real potential and innovation. This drive develops organizational character and guides organizational activity. Cooper reasons that leaders who exhibit these three traits are able to produce increases in emotional literacy, emotional fitness, emotional depth, and emotional alchemy.

The work of Covey and Goleman makes it clear that trait theory is not merely alive, but is thriving in significant ways. The relative simplicity of these and other popular conceptions, however, often obscures the inherent weakness of any trait approach: trait theory is exclusively leader-centered, and as such may have less actual utility and explanatory power than more recent theories.

SUMMARY

The trait approach represents the first attempt to develop leadership theory in a formal sense. Trait theories primarily focus on the leader and the characteristics and traits that seem to enable him or her to lead others. Whether or not these traits are based on learned or inherited skills, trait theorists believe that leaders bring certain abilities to the table that followers do not. Though it leaves a number of important questions unanswered, trait theory remains attractive to many because of its relative simplicity.

REFERENCES

Conger, J.A. and Kanungo, R.N. (1998). *Charismatic Leadership*. San Francisco: Jossey-Bass.

Cooper, R. K. (1997). "Applying emotional intelligence in the workplace." *Training & Development*, 51 (12), 31-39.

Covey, S. R. (1991). *Principle-centered leadership*. New York: Summit.

Goleman, D. (1998a). "Guidelines for best practice: How to improve emotional intelligence." *Training & Development*, 52 (10), 28-30.

Goleman, D. (1998b). "What makes a leader?" *Harvard Business Review*, (5), 93

House, R.J. (1977). "A 1976 Theory of Charismatic Leadership," in J.G. Hunt and L.L. Larson (eds.), *Leadership: The cutting edge*. pp. 189-207. Carbondale: Southern Illinois University.

Northouse, P.M. (1997). *Leadership: Theory and practice*. Thousand Oaks, CA: Sage Publications.

Stogdill, R.M. (1948). "Personal Factors Associated with Leadership: A Survey of the Literature." *Journal of Psychology*, 25, 35-71. Also (1974). *Handbook of Leadership: A survey of theory and research*. New York: Free Press.

Chapter 3   Name _____

DISCUSSION QUESTIONS

1. Discuss the basic premise behind the *great man* theory.

_____

_____

_____

_____

_____

_____

_____

2. List and discuss the key variables identified by Stogdill's 1948 Review.

_____

_____

_____

_____

_____

_____

_____

_____

_____

_____

_____

_____

_____

3. Discuss what you believe are the strengths and weaknesses of the trait approach to leadership.

_____

_____

_____

_____

_____

4. Discuss the key elements of charismatic leadership theory.

_____

_____

_____

_____

_____

_____

_____

5. Give an example of a charismatic leader. Explain why you chose this individual.

_____

_____

_____

_____

_____

_____

Chapter 3

Name _____

ACTIVITY

1. Think about a highly visible corporate leader who has impressed you. Also think of a political leader that has positively impressed you. Finally, think of a religious/spiritual leader that has helped you grow. Name the leaders you have chosen. Consider the traits of each of these leaders and compare each leader to the other based on their traits.

_____

_____

_____

_____

_____

_____

_____

_____

_____

_____

_____

_____

_____

_____

_____

_____

_____

CHAPTER 4

BEHAVIORAL THEORIES

Behavioral theories (sometimes referred to as "style" theories) are presented in this chapter. Pioneering work related to each of the three most commonly-identified styles of leadership are discussed: autocratic, democratic, and laissez-faire. Four leadership models are presented: the University of Michigan studies, Douglas McGregor's research, the Ohio State studies, and the Managerial Grid.

CHAPTER OBJECTIVES

After studying this chapter you should be able to:

√ define the autocratic, democratic, and laissez-faire styles of leadership, and discuss the pros and cons of each of these styles,

√ describe the studies conducted at the University of Michigan and the results,

√ understand the distinction between Theory X and Theory Y,

√ describe the development of the Two-Factor Theory at Ohio State University, and

√ discuss the Managerial Grid and identify and place the five anchor styles on the grid.

INTRODUCTION

When the search for a common trait or set of traits that could reliably predict leadership proved unproductive, the focus of researchers shifted to describing actions or behaviors that seemed essential to effective leadership. This shift in focus took some time, occurring over a span of many years. This new approach—the "behavioral" or "style" approach—became prominent after mid-century.

What do leaders actually do and how do they do it?

The behavioral approach is characterized by its goal of cataloging leader behaviors: what do leaders actually do and how do they do it? Instead of searching for the traits or characteristics that define leadership, this approach seeks to identify those behaviors that will have a positive impact on the performance and satisfaction of the followers. A major objective of this research is to determine whether a particular style or pattern of behaviors can be shown to be superior to others in achieving group goals. An important practical implication of this approach is a shift away from the search for leaders who "have the right stuff" toward development of training programs to instruct leaders in the skills necessary for successful leadership.

EARLY BEHAVIORAL APPROACHES

In 1938, two researchers at the University of Iowa, Kurt Lewin and Ronald Lippitt published one of the earliest studies discussing different leadership styles. The following year, Lewin, Lippitt and Ralph White identified three basic styles of leadership: autocratic, democratic, and laissez-faire. The autocratic style uses formal rules and regulations to control activities and relationships. All decisions are made by the leader, and a clear distinction is made between followers and the leader. The democratic style adopts a collaborative approach. Follower involvement and participation are encouraged in decision-making. Interactive relationships are encouraged, and rules, procedures and policies are minimized. Laissez-faire, a French word taken from laissez (let) and faire (do), suggests the principle of non-interference. Leaders using this style do not intervene unless asked or invited to do so. There is sometimes little interaction between leaders and followers, such that leaders may almost be non-participants.

The three styles lie on a continuum, with autocratic and laissez-faire at the endpoints and democratic in the middle.

These three styles are defined along a continuum, with autocratic and laissez-faire at the endpoints and democratic in the middle.

$$\overleftarrow{\hspace{8cm}}\overrightarrow{\hspace{0cm}}$$

Autocratic	Democratic	Laissez-faire
Style	Style	Style

Lewin, Lippitt and White's classic study of leadership styles observed four comparable groups of ten-year-old boys working on craft projects, such as making paper masks. Each group of boys was led by an adult who had been trained to use all three styles: autocratic, democratic, and laissez-faire. The boys met successively for three six-week periods with leaders using each style. The results of the study can be summarized as follows:

- Laissez-faire leaders were not as productive as democratic or autocratic leaders.
- Quality of work was poor under laissez-faire leadership.
- Satisfaction was low under laissez-faire leadership.
- Productivity was similar between autocratic and democratic groups while in the presence of the leader.
- When the respective leaders were called away, productivity dropped drastically in the autocratically-led group, but remained steady in the democratically-led groups.
- There was more aggressive and hostile behavior toward both leaders and group members in autocratically-led groups.
- Followers in the autocratic groups exhibited greater levels of dependence and less individuality as compared to those in democratic groups.
- There was greater commitment and cohesiveness among members of the democratic groups.

Additional Findings

Lewin, Lippitt and White reached additional conclusions with regard to each of the three leadership styles. Leaders who adopt an authoritarian style can expect:

- high productivity, increased hostility, aggression, and discontent as well as decreased commitment, independence, and creativity among followers.
- relative success with tasks requiring standard procedures and minimal commitment or initiative.
- relative success with routine, highly structured, or simple tasks.
- relative success when a leader is much more knowledgeable than his or her followers, when groups of followers are extremely large, or when there is insufficient time to engage in

democratic decision-making. (Military leaders, for example, dare not take time while under enemy fire to discuss the pros and cons of advancing or retreating.)

A leader adopting the democratic style can expect:

- relatively high productivity that contributes to increased satisfaction, commitment, and cohesiveness.
- relative success with tasks that require participation, involvement, creativity, and commitment to decisions.
- to encounter some difficulties related to time management and the complexities of group processes.

A leader adopting the laissez-faire style can expect:

- to spend less time actually engaged in leadership.
- decreased productivity and less satisfaction on the part of most followers.
- less innovation and creativity from followers.
- relative success and effectiveness with groups containing motivated and knowledgeable experts. (Such groups often do not require direct guidance and produce better results when left alone.)

The democratic style is best suited for tasks that require participation, involvement, creativity, and commitment to decisions.

University of Michigan Studies

Building on the work of Lewin, Lippett, and White, a massive effort led by Rensis Likert was undertaken at the University of Michigan in the early 1960's. Evidence from more than 500 studies was assimilated examining the effectiveness of autocratic leadership compared to democratic leadership. The following variables were used to measure effectiveness:

- costs
- worker satisfaction
- turnover
- absenteeism

- output per hour
- grievance rate
- scrap rate

Combining the results of his own research and the work of Lewin, Lippett, and White, Likert (1961) formulated four systems of interpersonal relations in large organizations:

System 1 ....Exploitative autocratic
System 2 ....Benevolent autocratic
System 3 ....Consultative
System 4 ....Democratic

The leadership behaviors of the System 1 (exploitative autocratic) leaders emphasize control by using fear, threats and punishment. Communication is one-way, from the leader to the follower. Decision-making and goal-setting is strictly in the hands of leaders, who assume positions distant from and superior to workers in their groups. System 4 (democratic) leaders are very supportive and encourage communication. These leaders solicit ideas and suggestion, and use a participative style in decision-making, emphasizing team approaches. Systems 2 and 3 (benevolent autocratic and consultative) represent two forms of compromise between the two endpoints on the continuum.

Democratic leaders will have better long-term results and more satisfied workers.

Using this continuum to analyze the 500 studies mentioned above, Likert concluded that "positive associations generally have been found between measures of the organization's performance and whether they are closer to democratic systems 3 and 4 than to autocratic systems 1 and 2" (Bass, 1990).

Other researchers since Likert have employed similar, single continuum approaches, but used somewhat different labeling for the endpoints. Some of the more common terms are listed below.

Autocratic	**Democratic**
Production oriented	Employee oriented
Job centered	Employee centered
Autocratic	Participative
Task oriented	Socio-emotional oriented

In sum, researchers using this approach understand the endpoints of their continuums as opposing styles of behavior. Conclusions generally suggest that leaders choosing more democratic styles will achieve better long-term results and have more satisfied employees.

MCGREGOR THEORY X AND THEORY Y

Designing work with a Theory Y view gives workers the freedom to achieve at their highest potential.

In the 1950s, Douglas McGregor postulated two alternative views of human motivation, Theory X and Theory Y. Theory X analyzed motivation on the basis of the assumption that humans are by nature essentially lazy, stupid, apathetic, and irresponsible; that they disdain work and will therefore do whatever they can to avoid it. McGregor believed that leaders who view human nature in this way will logically seek to design control devices that closely monitor and control human behavior. The (assumed) lack of ambition and indifference to organizational goals would necessitate directive, autocratic leadership. Workers would have to be coerced, controlled, and threatened in order to achieve organizational objectives. Indeed, Theory X seems to have been the operative paradigm in the design and management of work processes prior to McGregor's writing. Work was typically reduced to its simplest form so that supervisors could easily direct and control workers. Supervisors would plan the work, assign the work, direct the work, and measure work performance. Workers merely needed to do what they were told.

Theory Y, as proposed by McGregor, is the antithesis to Theory X. It assumes that work is as natural as play, and views workers as individuals who are willing to work hard, able to exercise self-direction, and eager to accept responsibility when they share a commitment to organizational goals. This view suggests that managers should design work in such a way that workers are granted maximum autonomy, recognition, and responsibility. Work processes that are designed from the standpoint of Theory Y attempt to give employees the freedom to achieve at their highest potential.

TWO-FACTOR APPROACHES

"Are the two dimensions at the endpoints of the continuum mutually exclusive?"

These one-dimensional (linear continuum) approaches were quickly followed by two-factor theories. Two-factor approaches question the assumption that the two dimensions at the endpoints of the continuum are mutually exclusive. Two-factor approaches suggest that a leader can use a production or task orientation to achieve goals while at the same time seeking to build a strong relationship with group members—a socio-emotional orientation. The Ohio State Leadership Studies and the Managerial Grid best exemplify this concept.

Ohio State Leadership Studies

An important leadership research program was undertaken at Ohio State University concurrently with the Michigan studies. The principle researchers were J.K. Hemphill, Ralph Stogdill, and Edwin Fleishman. Their goal was to identify basic types of behaviors that were universally used by leaders. Beginning with 1,800 descriptions of leader behavior, the researchers used statistical processes to distill these down to 150 descriptions of good leader behavior. These were in turn used to develop a research instrument called the Leadership Behavior Description Questionnaire (LBDQ). The initial study administered the LBDQ to aircrews, who were asked to use it to score their commanders. Statistical analysis of this data indicated two dimensions of leadership behavior: "consideration" and "initiating structure".

Consideration consisted of:

- building friendships
- mutual trust
- interpersonal respect
- warm working relationships
- two-way communication
- openness to followers' ideas and suggestions

Initiating structure referred to directing group activities through:

- planning
- scheduling
- encouraging standards of performance
- making task assignments
- emphasizing deadlines
- organizing the work

Consideration and initiating structure were viewed as independent dimensions of leadership. A leader could be high on consideration and low on initiating structure, or vice versa. It was also possible to be high or low on both dimensions. If the research discovered a positive relationship between group productivity and leaders who were high in both consideration and initiating structure, the findings would suggest that leaders should be trained in the skills of both dimensions, rather than just one.

Blake and Mouton's Managerial Grid

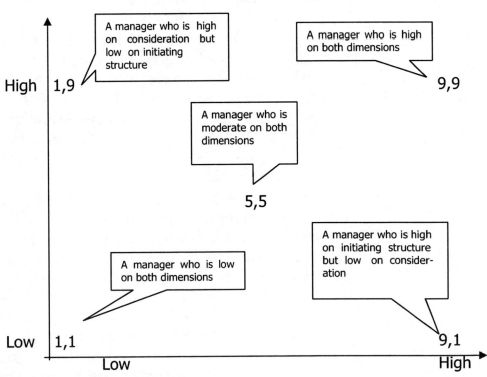

Blake and Mouton's Managerial Grid

Perhaps the best known of the two-factor approaches is Robert Blake and Jane Mouton's "Leadership Grid" (1964). Their model was built upon the work of both the Michigan and Ohio State studies. Much of the popularity of this model is due to its commercial training emphasis. Managers are able to score themselves on two dimensions: concern for production and concern for people. Each axis is divided into equally distant points from one to nine. Although a leader might find his or her score anywhere on the grid, five styles have been identified that act as anchors. The five plotted styles are defined and presented in a graphic form below:

(1,1) Impoverished Management. The impoverished leader demonstrated a low concern for tasks and a low concern for relationships. The leader with a (1,1) orientation does not actively attempt to influence others, but rather assigns responsibilities and leaves followers to complete tasks on their own.

(9,1) Authority-Obedience. This leader is very concerned with the completion of task assignments, but demonstrates little concern for personal relationships. The primary function of the (9,1) oriented leader is to plan, direct, and control behavior. Followers are viewed as human resources that facilitate the completion of tasks. Input from followers is not sought. A (9,1) oriented leader prefers to dominate decision-making.

(5,5) Organization Man Management. This middle-of-the-road leader is adequately concerned with production and people. In an attempt to involve followers, the (5,5) leader engages in compromise. Organization man leaders do not rock the boat – they push enough to achieve adequate productivity, but yield if they believe increasing the workload will strain interpersonal relationships. As a result, a (5,5) leader often achieves only mediocre results.

(1,9) Country Club Management. The country club leader is more concerned with interpersonal relationships than with the completion of tasks. The (1,9) leader seeks to establish a supportive, friendly environment. Although country club leaders may want tasks to be completed effectively, they emphasize factors that contribute to the personal satisfaction and happiness of followers. The (1,9) leader sees his or her primary responsibility as providing a positive working environment.

(9,9) Team Management. Team leadership involves a high concern for both production and people. The (9,9) leadership style is the ideal, for it emphasizes both successful execution of task

assignments and supportive concern for individuals. The (9,9) leader nurtures followers so that they are able to achieve excellence in both personal and team goals. Under team leadership, both leaders and followers work together to achieve the highest level of productivity and personal accomplishment.

SUMMARY

In spite of the intuitive attractiveness of a single style or set of behaviors that result in both goal attainment and human concern, research findings are inconclusive. A particular set of ideal behavioral styles has been as elusive as a particular set of ideal traits. But considerable evidence does suggest that different situations call for differing styles of leadership.

REFERENCES

Blake, R.R., and Mouton, J.S. (1964). *The managerial grid.* Houston, TX: Gulf.

Coch, L., and French, J.R.P. (1948). "Overcoming resistance to change." *Human Relations,* 1, 512-532.

Fleishman, E.A. (1953a). "The measurement of leadership attitudes in industry." *Journal of Applied Psychology.* 37, 153-158.

Fleishman, E.A. (1973). "Twenty years of consideration and structure." In E.A. Fleishman and J. G. Hunt (Eds.), *Current developments in the study of leadership.* Carbondale: Southern Illinois University Press.

Hare, A.P. (1953). "Small group discussions with participatory and supervisory leadership." *Journal of Abnormal and Social Psychology,* 48, 273-275.

Hemphill, J.K. (1950a). *Leader behavior description.* Columbus: Ohio State University, Personnel Research Board.

Lewin, K. and Lippitt, R. (1938). "An experimental approach to the study of autocracy and democracy: A preliminary note." *Sociometry, 1,* 292-300.

Lewin, K., Lippitt, R. and White, R.K. (1939). "Patterns of aggressive behavior in experimentally created social climates." *Journal of Social Psychology, 10,* 271-301.

Likert, R. (1961a). *New patterns of management.* New York: McGraw-Hill.

Likert, R. (1961b). "An emerging theory of organizations, leadership and management." In L. Petrullo & B.M. Bass (Eds.), *Leadership and Interpersonal Behavior.* New York: Holt, Rinehart & Winston.

Shaw, M. E. (1955). "A comparison of two types of leadership in various communication nets." *Journal of Abnormal and Social Psychology, 50,* 127-134.

Stogdill, R.M. (1963a). *Manual for the leader behavior description questionnaire – Form XII.* Columbus: Ohio State University, Bureau of Business Research.

Wischmeier, R.R. (1955). "Group-centered and leader-centered leadership: An experimental study." *Speech Monographs, 22,* 43-48.

Chapter 4   **Name** _____

DISCUSSION QUESTIONS

1. Describe the characteristics of:

Autocratic style leaders:_____

_____

_____

_____

_____

_____

Democratic style leaders:_____

_____

_____

_____

_____

_____

_____

Laissez-faire style leaders:_____

_____

_____

_____

_____

_____

_____

2. What results do each of these styles produce?_____

_____

_____

_____

_____

_____

_____

_____

_____

_____

_____

_____

3. What results do they have on member satisfaction? _____

_____

_____

_____

_____

_____

_____

_____

4. Define initiating structure and initiating consideration.

_____

_____

_____

_____

_____

_____

_____

_____

_____

_____

5. Compare and contrast the findings of the studies at the University of Michigan, Ohio State University, and the Managerial Grid.

_____

_____

_____

_____

_____

_____

_____

_____

_____

_____

Chapter 4

Name _____

ACTIVITY

In the course of your life, you have probably encountered individuals who tried to use each of the three styles of leadership mentioned in the chapter. Briefly describe one such encounter you can remember for each style, tell how you felt about that leadership style, and explain how it affected the group's ability to reach its goals.

Autocratic	
Democratic	
Laissez-faire	

CHAPTER 5

CONTINGENCY AND SITUATIONAL THEORIES

Contingency models have had a significant impact on the study of leadership. Fiedler's Contingency Theory centered on leader orientation (task or relationship) and situation favorableness. House's Path-Goal Theory focused on the factors that influence overall goal achievement. Hersey and Blanchard's Situational Leadership Theory considered the relationship between worker readiness and leadership style. Contingency models have been influential in the field and are still highly regarded today.

CHAPTER OBJECTIVES

After studying this chapter you should be able to:

√ explain Fiedler's contingency model of leadership,

√ describe the least-preferred co-worker scale and how it reveals leader orientation,

√ identify and describe the three components of situational favorableness,

√ discuss the match of LPC scores and situational favorableness for most effective leadership performance,

√ explain the Path-Goal theory of leadership, and

√ describe Hersey and Blanchard's leadership model.

INTRODUCTION

Trait and behavioral theorists both seek to identify traits or styles that best predict successful leadership. Because the results of these approaches have been mixed and inconclusive, researchers have looked for new approaches. Most theorists now agree that effective leadership is a complex process that cannot be attributed to a single trait or style that is best in all situations. Early researchers tried to ignore situational variables or to hold them constant, but it is now believed that situational variables led to the mixed results of such research. The situational characteristics that may influence leadership effectiveness include:

It became apparent that effective leadership was a complex process that could not be attributed to a single trait or style that was best in all situations.

- the personal characteristics of followers,
- task factors, and
- organizational factors.

This chapter discusses three theories that incorporate these important situational variables: Fiedler's Contingency Model, House's Path-Goal Theory, and Hersey and Blanchard's Situational Leadership Theory. The basic premise of all three theories is that the best or most effective leadership style or trait depends on the situation. In other words, results are contingent upon—they depend upon—the situation.

FIEDLER'S CONTINGENCY MODEL

Fred Fiedler's (1967) contingency model is the earliest and most widely studied of the contingency theories. His theory matches the leader's personality or style with the degree of situational control or influence. The beginning point in this process is determining the leader's least-preferred co-worker score (LPC). The LPC scale is a projective technique, similar to a Rorschach inkblot test. On the surface, this appears to involve evaluating a past co-worker, but it in fact reveals one's own personality or style. The LPC asks leaders to describe their least-preferred co-worker using a list of eight-point, bipolar adjective sets.

Four examples of the bipolar adjective sets follow:

Pleasant	8	7	6	5	4	3	2	1	Unpleasant
Friendly	8	7	6	5	4	3	2	1	Unfriendly
Inefficient	1	2	3	4	5	6	7	8	Efficient
Boring		1	2	3	4	5	6	7	8	Interesting

The scores are summed for the entire list to determine a leader's LPC score. Leaders with low LPC scores rate their least-preferred co-worker in more negative terms and are classified as task-oriented leaders. Leaders with high LPC scores use more positive terms and are classified as relationship-oriented leaders. A leader's LPC score is indicative of a relatively consistent characteristic that does not easily change. This theory, therefore, does not see leaders as highly malleable.

Situation Favorableness

Fiedler proposed an eight-octant continuum of situational favorableness. One endpoint represents a situation that affords the leader a great deal of control and influence. The other endpoint represents the opposite, a situation affording little control or influence. Three variables combine to define situational favorableness: leader-member relations, task structure, and power position. Leader-member relations describes how well the leader gets along with the group. Is the relationship cooperative and friendly, and does the leader feel support and loyalty from followers? Task structure has to do with how well the group's task is defined. Task structure is highest when a goal is clear to all and there seems to be one obvious path to achieve the goal. Task structure becomes lower as tasks become more ambiguous and the number of potential avenues to goal attainment increase. Position power is defined by the formal authority given to the leader. An officer in the military would have very strong position power, as opposed to a student chairing an all-volunteer committee on campus beautification, who would have relatively weak position power.

Leader-member relations is the strongest of the three variables and position power is the weakest.

These three variables do not play equal roles in determining situational favorableness. Leader-member relations is the most influential, and position power is the least influential. Fiedler developed the continuum of situational favorableness and its eight octants so as to incorporate every possible combination of the three variables. The table on the next page shows the eight possible combinations of the variables. Together these constitute the continuum of situational favorableness.

The situation in octant 1 is the most favorable, with good leader-member relations, high task structure, and strong position power. Octant 8, on the other hand, is the most unfavorable situation with poor leader-member relations, low task structure, and weak position power.

Fiedler's Contingency Model

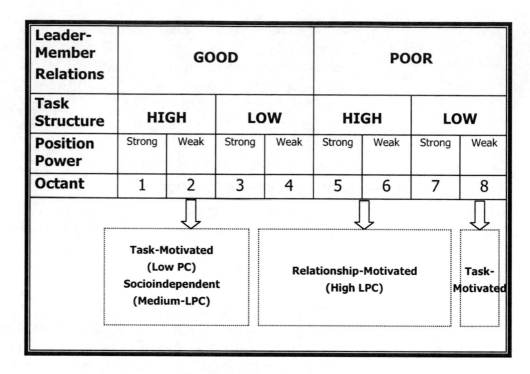

Leader-Member Relations	GOOD				POOR			
Task Structure	HIGH		LOW		HIGH		LOW	
Position Power	Strong	Weak	Strong	Weak	Strong	Weak	Strong	Weak
Octant	1	2	3	4	5	6	7	8

Task-Motivated (Low PC) Socioindependent (Medium-LPC)

Relationship-Motivated (High LPC)

Task-Motivated

Research Results

The next step this research approach matches leaders' LPC scores with situational favorableness and with a measure of effectiveness. Fiedler and his associates conducted a huge number of studies, examining a variety of situations ranging from military units to basketball teams. The correlation between LPC scores and group performance was plotted for each octant. Results indicated that leaders with low LPC scores (task-oriented leaders) are more effective in situations that are very favorable or very unfavorable, as represented by octants 1, 2, 3, and 8. High LPC leaders (relationship-oriented leaders) are most successful in situations that are moderately favorable, represented by octants 4, 5, 6, and 7.

Critique of Fiedler's Model

As noted earlier, Fiedler's Contingency Model has been widely researched and replicated. Not all of this research has been supportive of the model. The use of the LPC scale to measure leadership style has been criticized in several cases (Singh, 1983; Shiflett, 1981; Kennedy, 1982; Rice, 1978b). Researchers have also criticized the methods used to define situational favorableness (Vecchio, 1977; Jago and Ragan, 1986). These criticisms, however, do not detract from the impact Fiedler's Model has had on the study of leadership. His model is the most complete, best-validated theory in the leadership literature. Strube and Garcia (1981) reviewed well over 100 different studies that used Fiedler's model. Most of the studies supported his theoretical assumptions.

Concerns have been expressed about the practicality of Fiedler's approach, for its complexity might discourage practitioners who attempt to apply it in particular situations. For example, what if there is a mismatch between the leader and the situation? What should a high LPC leader do when faced with an octant 1 situation? Fiedler attempted to address this concern. Because he felt that LPC score measured a relatively permanent characteristic, it did not follow that a leader could attend a training program to change his or her style or LPC score. But this did not preclude the leader from "re-engineering the job" to fit his or her style (Fiedler, 1965). Fiedler provided practical suggestions to help leaders be more effective. These are outlined below.

Fiedler's theory is complex, and could discourage some practitioners.

Because leader-member relations is the most determinative variable, this is the first area to address. To improve leader-member relations, leaders should:

- spend more – or less – informal time with subordinates (lunch, leisure activities, and so on).
- request that particular people join their group.
- volunteer to direct difficult or troublesome subordinates.
- suggest transfers of particular subordinates out of their group.
- raise morale by obtaining positive outcomes for subordinates (special bonuses, time off, attractive assignments, and so on).

After leader-member relations, task structure is the next most important determinant of effective leadership. To develop skill in handling less structured tasks:

- ask your superior to give you the new or unusual problems whenever possible and allow you to figure out how to solve them.
- bring problems and tasks to group members, and invite them to work with you to structure those tasks.

The final component of leadership, according to Fiedler, is the position power of the leader. To increase position power:

- show subordinates who is boss by fully exercising your formal powers.
- Make sure that relevant information gets channeled to your group.

  To reduce your position power:
- call on members of your group to participate in planning and decision-making functions.
- allow subordinates to exercise relatively more power.

PATH-GOAL THEORY

R.J. House's "path-goal theory" is rooted in expectancy motivation theory (1971). Expectancy theory postulated that an individual's motivation level was a function of three variables: expectancy (if I put forth the effort, can I achieve the goal?); instrumentality (if I achieve the goal, will there be a reward?); and valance (how much do I value the reward?).

Path-Goal theory primarily focuses on how leaders can increase follower motivation by clearing the path to a goal and ensuring desired rewards for goal attainment. Effective leaders:

- help to clarify expectations
- identify the path to goal attainment
- provide necessary tools, training, and information
- help to establish goals
- link performance to expected outcome (pay raise, recognition, promotion)

> *Path-Goal theory addresses how leaders can increase follower motivation by clearing the path to a goal and ensuring desired rewards for goal attainment.*

Quality leadership entails acting as a catalyst by raising the expectations of followers and ensuring a highly valued reward when goals are reached. Over time, path-goal was modified to account for the ways leadership style interacted with two contingency factors: characteristics of followers, and characteristics of situations (House, 1971). Path-goal theory identifies four styles of behavior that leaders might adopt.

- *Directive* leaders provide structure by establishing work schedules, developing procedures and rules, making plans, organizing and setting policy, and making unilateral decisions.

- *Supportive leaders* still maintain control of work processes, but use a courteous and friendly style, offering lots of support to followers so as to create a positive work climate.

- *Participative leaders* use a consultative approach. Input from followers is encouraged, and suggestions, concerns and recommendations are welcomed.

- *Achievement-Oriented leaders* set challenging goals and stress excellence while demonstrating confidence in followers' abilities.

House's Path - Goal Theory

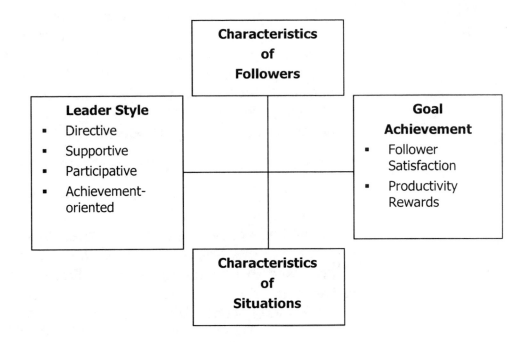

Beliefs about how readily a leader can change his or her style represent a critical difference between path-goal theory and Fiedler's contingency model. Remember that Fiedler felt a leader's style was essentially unchangeable. Path-goal theory makes a very different assumption. Leaders are seen as not only having the ability to change styles, but also as having an obligation to do so in order to use whatever style best fits the situation. Two contingency factors influence the selection of the appropriate leadership style: characteristics of followers, and characteristics of situations. Follower characteristics include work experience, needs (safety, esteem, belongingness), and personality (self-esteem, locus of control, introversion/ extroversion). Situational characteristics include task structure (routine/non-routine, skill level), formal authority system, and the nature of the work group.

The leader selects the appropriate style depending on whom they are leading and what they are doing.

Leaders select appropriate styles depending on whom they are leading and what they are doing. Workers who are inexperienced and unsure of themselves find a more directive style reassuring and satisfying. Experienced, skilled workers, on the other hand, would find a directive style annoying. Followers with low self-esteem will fit better with a leader using a supportive style. Those with high self-esteem will flourish with an achievement-oriented style.

Research Findings

Extensive research has been done to test path-goal theory, but findings have not been as supportive or consistent as work done to test Fiedler's model (Wofford & Liska, 1993; House & Dressler, 1974). But though research findings have been mixed, path-goal theory has provided a conceptual framework useful in understanding the relationship between leader styles, follower needs, and situational characteristics.

THE SITUATIONAL LEADERSHIP MODEL

Hersey and Blanchard (1969) used the Ohio State studies as the foundation for their Situational Leadership Theory (SLT). This model has not been extensively researched, but has become very popular in industrial management training programs. As previously discussed in Chapter 4, the Ohio State studies had developed a two-dimensional model, one dimension being initiating structure (task orientation), the other being consideration (relationship behavior). The SLT extends the Ohio State model to include the maturity level of followers. The model maintains that the best leadership style is contingent on the maturity level of workers.

SLT maintains that the best leadership style is contingent on the maturity level of workers.

SLT proposes the concept of follower readiness as defined by the followers' job maturity and psychological maturity relative to a specific task. Job maturity refers to the abilities, skills and knowledge that followers bring to a task. Psychological maturity has to do with the level of self-confidence and motivation followers have relative to the task. Job maturity and psychological maturity can be combined to produce a scale with four quadrants, or "readiness levels". The grid is then divided into four additional quadrants indicating different styles of leadership. SLT then seeks to match follower readiness with the appropriate leadership style:

Level One -- R1, S1: When followers are immature (R1), the appropriate style is telling (S1). Leaders structure tasks by making all decisions as to who should do what, where, and when. They also provide clear, specific instructions.

Level Two – R2, S2: If followers are moderately immature (R2), the appropriate style is selling (S2). Leaders still need to provide a high level of structure, but greater emphasis is placed on being supportive, explaining decisions, building confidence, and offering opportunity for clarification.

Level Three – R3, S3: When followers are moderately mature (R3), the appropriate style is participating (S3). Leaders share ideas and use joint decision-making. The more followers participate in designing tasks, the more willing they will be to execute those tasks.

Level Four – R4, S4: When followers are mature (R4), leaders should use delegation (S4). The followers know what needs to be done, know how to do it, and are motivated to do it. Leaders should delegate responsibility and allow followers to operate freely.

Hersey & Blanchard's Situational Model

Readiness Level	Leadership Style
R1–Readiness Level 1: Low job maturity and low psychological maturity (low task skills and low motivation).	**S1-Telling**: High task orientation, low relationship behavior.
R2–Readiness Level 2: Low job maturity and high psychological maturity (low task skills, but high motivation).	**S2-Selling**: High task orientation, high relationship behavior.
R3–Readiness Level 3: High job maturity and low psychological maturity (high task skills, but low motivation).	**S3-Participating**: Low task orientation, high relationship behavior.
R4–Readiness Level 4: High job maturity and high psychological maturity (high task skills and high motivation).	**S4-Delegating**: Low task orientation, low relationship behavior.

This model assumes that leaders are flexible in terms of the style they use. This flexibility is essential, because as a team moves from one task to another, its maturity level will fluctuate. For example, a carpenter doing volunteer remodeling at his church may be very mature relative to that task, but relatively immature when serving on the youth counseling committee. Although the SLT is not extensively supported by other research, it is very appealing to corporate trainers who need a conceptual foundation for leadership training programs.

SUMMARY

To date, contingency theories provide the richest source of data relative to our understanding of leadership. Fiedler's contingency theory, House's path-goal theory, and Hersey and Blanchard's situational leadership model all explore the importance of situations, and how situational variations interact with leader style in determining leadership effectiveness. Though these theorists employ different methods and different assumptions, particularly with respect to leader flexibility, all assume that effectiveness is contingent upon the situation.

REFERENCES

Fiedler, F.E. (1965). "Engineering the job to fit the manager." *Harvard Business Review, 43(5),* 115-122.

Fiedler, F.E. (1967). *A theory of leadership effectiveness.* New York: McGraw-Hill.

Hersey and Blanchard (1969).

House, R.J. (1971). "A path goal theory of leader effectiveness." *Administrative Science Quarterly, 16,* 321-338.

Jago, A.G. and Ragan, J.W. (1986a). "The trouble with LEADER MATCH is that it doesn't match Fiedler's contingency model." *Journal of Applied Psychology. 71,* 555-559.

Kennedy, J.K. (1982). "Middle LPC leaders and the contingency model of leadership effectiveness." *Organizational Behavior and Human Performance, 30,* 1-14.

Rice, R.W. (1978b). "Construct validity of the least preferred co-worker score." *Psychology Bulletin, 85,* 1199-1237.

Singh, R. (1983). "Leadership style and reward allocation: Does least preferred co-worker scale measure task and relation orientation?" *Organizational Behavior and Human Performance, 32(2),* 178-197.

Chapter 5   Name _____

DISCUSSION QUESTIONS

1. When would you select a task-oriented style of leadership?

_____

_____

_____

_____

_____

2. When would you select a relationship-oriented style of leadership? _____

_____

_____

_____

_____

_____

3. Explain what Fiedler's LPC scale is designed to measure.

_____

_____

_____

_____

_____

_____

4. Identify and describe the three components of situational favorableness.

_____

_____

_____

_____

_____

_____

_____

5. Describe the path-goal theory of leadership.

_____

_____

_____

_____

_____

_____

6. Discuss Hersey and Blanchard's situational leadership model.

_____

_____

_____

_____

_____

_____

Chapter 5	Name _____

CASE STUDY

Read the following case study and analyze the leadership involved from the perspective of the Situational Leadership Model.

CJ Smith and Jake Miller have been friends a long time. They started at **The Lumber Rack** about 5 years ago and have worked side by side in the yard. About a year ago, CJ was promoted to yard foreman, due to the fact that he had more prior experience in lumberyards than Jake did. Due to the growth of the company, three months ago CJ was given permission to hire a new yard person. While Jake is a dependable, solid worker with much knowledge, the new hire, Chad, is younger and has more energy (but little patience). There have been some tense moments in the yard as Jake and Chad have argued about the "right" way to do something. Jake likes the way the yard has been organized, but Chad would like to see major changes in the way inventory is stocked. CJ has been asked to step in and provide leadership in helping the yard become a "team" capable of accommodating the rapid growth of **The Lumber Rack**. CJ is ready to take on the challenge, but is not sure how to proceed.

1. What leadership style would best motivate Jake? Explain why.

_____

_____

_____

_____

_____

_____

2. What leadership style should be used for Chad? Explain why.

_____

_____

_____

_____

_____

_____

3. What actions should CJ take to address the concerns of each individual?

_____

_____

_____

_____

_____

_____

_____

_____

_____

4. What could be done using a team approach to successfully handle this situation?

_____

_____

_____

_____

_____

_____

_____

_____

_____

CHAPTER **6**

POWER AND INFLUENCE THEORIES

Trait, behavioral, and contingency theories all attempt to isolate important characteristics of leaders, followers, or situations. Leadership is thus seen as something of a scientific process of measuring and manipulating these variables to improve outcomes. Theories centering on power and influence fit into this category as well, for they view power as the most important characteristic of both leaders and followers, and as the key to leadership effectiveness. In this chapter, power is defined and several types of power are explained. The methods and processes of influence are considered in the context of the leader-follower relationship, and the concepts and principles of empowerment are introduced.

CHAPTER OBJECTIVES

After studying this chapter you should be able to:

√ understand the role of power in organizations,

√ explain the five types and sources of power and list several sources of organizational power,

√ understand social exchange theory and the benefits and costs of power,

√ define influence and recognize its importance,

√ distinguish ethical from unethical influence,

√ understand empowerment and its advantages/disadvantages, and

√ list several principles that guide effective empowerment.

INTRODUCTION

Whether in a leadership role or not, everyone uses power and influence in some form or another. But power and influence are vital elements in any effective leadership relationship, though they are often confused with one another. Classical leadership viewed power as the single means of gaining the compliance of followers. Progressive leadership generally sees influence as the more appropriate device. It is no surprise, therefore, that people confuse the two or are unable to clearly explain the differences between them. Consider these two workplace scenarios.

Fred Thomas has been a clerk for six months at Ace Department Store. He walks into the manager's office early on a Monday morning, and is greeted by his manager and co-workers. They begin to discuss the tasks that need completion. Together the team develops a list of projects for the day and the week. By 9 a.m., Fred is working on the first project from the list. Later, Fred's manager, Bill, comes up to him and asks him to start another project. Bill proceeds to explain to Fred that the additional project is more pressing and needs attention. Fred complies, immediately dropping what he is doing to pick up the other project. He has it finished by lunchtime.

Tom Frederick has been a store clerk for Acme Lumber for two years. He walks into the office on a Monday morning ready to start the week. Tom is given a list of tasks to perform for the day, just as he is every day. Tom begins on the first project and after an hour his manager, Bob, tells him to stop working on that project and begin working on another one. Tom complies, but asks Bob what he should do about the first project. Bob suggests that Tom need only worry about this new project now and can go back to his other project later. Tom completes the new project just before quitting time and leaves his original project for the next day.

ELEMENTS OF POWER

Every use of power brings with it a cost.

The simple use or abuse of power has long been confused with leadership. Individuals with the ability to wield brute power have generally been seen as successful "leaders". Today, our society seems to have a love-hate relationship with power. People want leaders who take charge, but resent leaders on "power trips" or who are "control freaks".

In an organizational setting, power has been defined in a number of ways. In the context of leadership, power might be understood as the ability to control the behavior of others. Power might then involve manipulating another person to bring about a desired behavior, or allocating resources in a manner designed to change another's behavior. Using power in such ways means that others are goaded, pushed, or coerced into behaving in a certain manner against their will.

A person does not hold power independently, for power implies a relationship between people. Power does not exist unless there are people who can perceive and be subject to that power. Power is, in this sense, a transaction between people, and as in any transaction, every exercise of power involves a cost. Sometimes the person wielding power is not concerned with that cost; he or she primarily desires control of the situation. In such cases, it might be said that the person has been "blinded by their power".

It is interesting to ask why people allow themselves to be controlled. Even if an individual in control in fact has relatively limited power, most of us have been conditioned to obey instructions. We have what can be called a "zone of indifference". The zone of indifference is the range of requests to which a person is likely to obey without feeling stress. Some people have larger zones of indifference, which indicates a broader range of behaviors they would engage in for others without stress. For persons with a smaller zone of indifference, the range of acceptable behavior is more limited.

Types of Power

In 1959, French and Raven identified sources of social power separated into two distinct categories: position power and personal power. Position power relates to power that emanates from the resources or formal organizational authority a person holds. Because it involves more transactional behaviors, position power is generally considered to be a less mature form of power. Personal power emerges from the personality of the leader and the technical or interpersonal skills they possess.

Those experienced in leadership often resort to the use of personal power rather than position power.

Experienced leaders prefer to use personal power rather than position power. Both of these power bases have been further categorized. Position power utilizes rewards, coercion, and legitimate authority, while forms of personal power include expert and referent power.

- *Reward*. Reward power is the ability to trade positive stimuli for a desired behavioral response from the subject. Persons holding this form of power are perceived as being able to mediate rewards. Reward power is commonly used in the workplace in the form of bonuses, promotions, and fringe benefits.

- *Coercive.* Coercive power is the ability to withhold negative consequences in return for a desired behavior. It is useful only when the subject believes that the controller actually possesses the ability to prevent the undesirable consequence. This type of power is commonly used in organizations in the form of demotion, reprimand, or termination.

- *Legitimate.* Legitimate power stems from the perception of authority or status in an organization or in society. Power in this sense is a product of position. Persons known to be senior managers, for example, are afforded more respect than are other employees. The respect shown to police or military officers, political leaders or clergy also exemplifies this type of power.

- *Expert.* Expert power derives from the perception that a person has expert knowledge about a particular relevant area. It produces credible leadership to a point –when expertness is not believed or not understood – then it serves no purpose. This type of power is exemplified when we search out experts for their particular skills, such as physicians, accountants, and lawyers.

- *Referent.* Referent power occurs when people develop strong bonds as a product of mutual respect for one another. This is also referred to as the power of friendship, and is perhaps the most mature form of power. (Referent power is capable of stimulating positive behaviors that other forms of power can not.) The cognitive equation looks something like this: *Benefits - Costs = Desirability of the outcome.* There may be very few things, for example, that someone is unlikely to do for their best friend.

Power can be derived from a variety of situations. Consider the following ways power can be created:

- power from ownership or investment
- power from popularity or charisma
- power from the possession of resources
- power from access to opportunities
- power from association

Each of these situations represent opportunities for individuals to leverage the friendships they have created or the rewards, punishments, authority or knowledge they control.

Although power is crucial to the effective functioning of organizations, potential pitfalls accompany the use of each of the five types of power. Use of position power can lead to a workplace characterized by mistrust and materialism. Both expert and referent power can fail to motivate followers if used inappropriately. Effective leaders seek to use the most mature form of power available given the particular characteristics of followers and situations.

Social Exchange Theory

Power and influence are rooted in processes of social exchange. Social exchange theory suggests two basic points. First, people engage in power exchanges knowing that some parties will benefit more than others. As people interact in power situations, they attempt to discern what they can and cannot expect to receive from a given exchange. People with more power are generally assumed to be able to get more out of an exchange than those holding less power. Persons with limited power may feel "railroaded" or forced to accept what those with more power are willing to give.

The second basic point is that participants in social exchange measure the desirability of outcomes by comparing the costs and benefits of using power. The potential benefits to be derived from the use of power must outweigh any potential cost. The cognitive equation looks something like this: *Benefits - Costs = Desirability of the outcome.*

"To some, power means control. To be powerful may feel heady, exhilarating, exciting. Some feel strong with it, and impotent without it."

Lee (1997)

Because the relationship between leaders and followers is mutual and reciprocal, social exchange theory assumes that when one party uses power, another party experiences a form of loss. There are costs associated with the loss. If a leader uses power to sway a decision, followers may band together to prevent the decision from being implemented if they perceive the costs to them as significant. The point is that even those people with less power have the ability to influence outcomes. There are almost always costs associated with the abuse of power.

Social exchange theory sees the leader/follower relationship as being based on mutual influence, even though one side may hold superior power. Consider the following benefits and costs of using different forms of power outlined in the chart on the following page.

Given the corresponding costs and benefits, social exchange theory suggests that leaders who use expert and referent power, and minimize the use of legitimate and coercive power, will be more effective. Leaders who employ legitimate and/or coercive power will incur higher costs, and in the end do more harm than good for the organization.

French & Raven's Five Types of Power

Power Type	Benefits	Costs
Reward	- May motivate effectively - Attracts attention to giver and receiver - Commonly used - May create helpful competition	- If rewards are not available, motivation decreases - Some may not perform up to expectations or may feel "used" or "cheap"
Coercive	- Should be used only as a last resort - Provides quick results - Useful for discipline	- Creates resentment and mistrust - Results diminish over time; provides only short-term effectiveness
Legitimate	- Culturally sanctioned - Users carry the status of the organization - Useful for discipline	- Short-term results may be fleeting if the authority figure leaves the organization - Lowers satisfaction
Expert	- Increased satisfaction - Enhanced performance - Few drawbacks	- May be perceived as "cocky" - Expert must have genuine knowledge - Not as useful for discipline
Referent	- Increased satisfaction - Enhanced performance - Few drawbacks	- Difficult to develop - Diminishes if overused - Not as useful for discipline

ELEMENTS OF INFLUENCE

The ability to exercise influence is one of the most important aspects of effective leadership. Leadership involves influence in that leaders are often called upon to modify the attitudes, behaviors, or values of followers. Such changes are in fact the primary goal of intentional influence, though unintentional influence can have similar results. These changes must come from the follower, however, and not from the leader. That is, followers must exercise free will in making the changes. If followers believe their free will has been violated, the leader's attempt to influence becomes an assertion of power. Free will can be defined as the perception that the follower has an actual choice that *he/she* can make. In the absence of free will, change occurs in response to power alone. Genuine influence stems from three basic sources: competency and knowledge, character and trust, and dynamism and charisma. To effectively influence others, therefore, leaders must demonstrate competency and trustworthiness. Followers, likewise, must do the same in order to influence their leaders.

Methods of Influence

Developed by Gary Yukl and his colleagues, the following list of 11 proactive influence tactics are relevant for influencing others.

Becoming adept at influencing others is hard work and the results may not be obvious, but for long-term organizational success, it is necessary.

Influence Tactics
Rational Persuasion: The agent uses logical arguments and factual evidence to show a request is relevant for attaining task objectives.
Apprising: The agent explains how carrying out a request or supporting a proposal will benefit the target personally or advance the target's career.
Inspirational Appeals: The agent makes an appeal seeking to arouse the target person's emotions to gain commitment for a request.
Consultation: The agent encourages the target to suggest improvements in a proposal, or to help plan an activity or change for which the target person's support and assistance are desired.
Exchange: The agent offers an incentive, an exchange of favors, or indicates willingness to reciprocate at a later time if the target will do the request.
Collaboration: The agent offers to provide relevant resources and assistance if the target will carry out a request or approve a proposed change.
Personal Appeal: The agent asks the target to carry out a request out of friendship, or asks for a personal favor before saying what it is.
Ingratiation: The agent uses praise or flattery before or during an influence attempt or expresses confidence in the target's ability.
Legitimating Tactics: The agent establishes legitimacy of a request or verifies authority by referring to rules, formal policies, or official documents.
Pressure: The agent uses demands, threats, or persistence to influence.
Coalition Tactics: The agent seeks the aid of others to persuade the target to do something or uses the support of others as a reason for compliance.

Empowerment as Influence

Empowerment can be defined as the process of motivating followers by giving *them* control over *their* projects. Empowerment represents a form of risk-taking on the part of leaders, even when followers are highly competent. Empowerment is substantially different from delegation, its older counterpart. Management literature has long touted the need for increased delegation of tasks. Giving work away makes sense for leaders who have more work than they can handle alone. Delegation differs from empowerment, however, in that managers who delegate retain decision-making authority and monitor most aspects of the work process. Delegation retains managerial control of projects, while empowerment pushes control down to the level where it really belongs, to those actually doing the work.

Advantages of Empowerment	Disadvantages of Empowerment
- Gives workers autonomy over projects - Reduces a leader's role in projects so he or she can concentrate on other projects - Creates satisfaction in followers - Produces higher drive for success and productivity - Ownership creates responsibility for the project - Desired outcomes are better defined - Creates a trusting and collaborative environment	- Takes control of project away from leader - Requires leader effort to initiate and maintain the empowerment process - Failure can be fatal for both employee and leader - May not always follow the project schedule - Followers may want additional power that is inappropriate - Can degenerate into chaos and irresponsible behavior

Empowerment became a popular buzzword in the 1990s, and much research has been done to explore and develop the concept. Actual empowerment, however, occurs much less often than we are given to think. Managers commonly endorse empowerment as a concept or strategy, but fail to follow through. Managers who are more honest admit that, even though they would like to be more empowering, their organizations are unwilling to risk the chance of failure. Because all organizations seek to maximize success and minimize failure, the perception of increased risk associated with empowerment is a disincentive for managers. But empowerment has distinct advantages over other strategies, and these should be given as much consideration as its disadvantages.

To increase the likelihood of success when using empowerment, consider the following principles:

- Negotiate responsibilities in the beginning.
- Give authority equal to the responsibilities negotiated.
- Communicate what is expected.
- Provide the information and resources necessary for success.
- Give feedback (positive and negative) on project activity.
- Trust project participants.
- Allow participants to do their best, even if the end result is failure.
- Demonstrate continuing respect for participants.

SUMMARY

Power and influence are essential components in the leadership relationship. Position power and personal power each have a place in that relationship. Leaders can effectively influence followers if they base that influence on mutual respect rather than on power differences between themselves and followers. Ethical leaders choose power and influence strategies that maximize the free will of followers. Empowerment has emerged as a popular strategy for sharing power, but the advantages and disadvantages of empowerment must be carefully considered.

REFERENCES

Barge, J. K. (1994). *Leadership: Communication skills for organizations and groups*. New York: St. Martin's.

Bass, B. M. (1985) *Leadership and performance beyond expectations*. New York: Free Press.

French, J. R. & Raven, B. (1959). *The bases of social power*, in *Studies in social power*. Ann Arbor, MI: University of Michigan Press.

Galbraith, J. K. (1983). *The anatomy of power*. Boston, MA: Houghton Mifflin.

Gardner, J. (1990). *On leadership*. New York: Free Press.

Greenleaf, R. K. (1977). *Servant leadership: A journey into the nature of legitimate power and greatness.* New York: Paulist Press.

Griffin, G. R. (1991) *Machiavelli on management: Playing and winning the corporate power game.* New York: Praeger.

Hackman, M. Z. & Johnson, C. E. (1996). Leadership: A communication perspective. Prospect Heights, IL: Waveland.

Hagberg, J. O. (1994). *Real power: Stages of personal power in organizations.* Salem, WI: Sheffield.

Lee, B. (1997). *The power principle.* New York: Simon and Schuster.

Pfeffer, J. (1992). *Managing with power: Politics and nfluence in organizations.* Boston, MA: Harvard Business School Press.

Potts, J. D. (2001). *The ethical difference: Why leaders are more than managers.* Longmont, CO: Rocky Mountain Press.

Tracy, D. (1990). *10 steps to empowerment.* New York: William Morrow & Co.

Trenholm, S. (1989). *Persuasion and social influence.* Englewood Cliffs, NJ: Prentice Hall

Yukl, G. A. (2002*). Leadership in organizations* (Fifth edition). Englewood Cliffs, NJ: Prentice Hall.

Chapter 6

DISCUSSION QUESTIONS

1. Discuss the differences between power, influence, and empowerment.

   _____

   _____

   _____

   _____

   _____

   _____

   _____

   _____

2. Using the following table, list advantages and disadvantages inherent in each method.

Method	Advantages	Disadvantages
Power		
Influence		
Empowerment		

3. Why do you think empowerment is not as widely used as power
    or influence?

    _____

    _____

    _____

    _____

    _____

    _____

    _____

    _____

    _____

    _____

    _____

    _____

    _____

    _____

    _____

    _____

    _____

    _____

    _____

    _____

Chapter 6	**Name** _____

CASE STUDY

Jim Braun is the president of the Student Oversight Group at Hanford College. The purpose of the Student Oversight Group is to handle problems that arise when students violate Hanford's academic or personal conduct codes. The SOG includes the following members:

Jim Braun	22/Senior	Bus. Admin./Acct.	President
Steve Baxter	21/Junior	Computer Science	Secretary
Sarah Homer	25/Junior	Social Work	Treasurer
Billi Schmidt	30/Senior	Physical Education	Member
Robert Smith	20/Sophomore	Graphic Design	Member
Brenda Moller	22/Senior	Accounting	Member
Dr. Sandra Hardin		History	Faculty Advisor

It is normal for problems to be referred to the SOG and resolved before official discipline is taken. The SOG attempts to handle all problems in a timely manner, then report their recommendation to the Dean for action. The SOG is an empowered task force with the duty to make decisions and have those decisions implemented in all but the rarest of situations. Hanford graduates are often offered the highest paying jobs in the market because of their skills.

Sometime during the winter break, between fall and spring semester, Jim's dorm room was broken into. The intruders took a few valuable items, including a clock radio, some books purchased for the spring semester, and his computer disks. One of the disks contained all the records (investigative information, minutes, and decisions) of the SOG. One of the pending cases was due for final hearing and the disk contained all of the investigation information. The case involved a violation of the alcohol code and involved Robert Smith's roommate Will Scott. Jim began investigating and found that there were only ten residents who had access to the dorm over the winter break. About a month passed, and no information surfaced about any of the missing items, except the SOG computer disk. Through other group members (Billi and Brenda), Jim heard that the disk was in Robert's possession. Billi and Brenda did not know if Robert was involved in the theft, but they were quite sure he now had the disk. There is a SOG meeting scheduled next Friday and Robert will be attending, as will Billi and Brenda. At that meeting, a ruling will be made regarding Will Scott's alcohol violation. Jim has spoken to the faculty advisor and has been informed that she will not be able to attend the meeting due to prior commitments out of town. In her absence, Jim has the full authority of the faculty advisor to discuss and make decisions regarding Will's violation.

How could power, influence, and empowerment be used together to resolve this case?

_____

_____

_____

CHAPTER 7

TRANSFORMATIONAL, CULTURAL, AND SYMBOLIC THEORIES

The theories of leadership reviewed in this chapter represent a qualitative shift away from the more or less empirical, scientific assumptions of classical theories. Instead of assuming that leadership is an equation or process involving certain variables, these progressive theories see leadership in terms of the meaning or value it creates or reinforces for a group or organization. In historical context, this shift in emphasis may have reflected growing disillusionment in the 60s and 70s with science and the fruit of the industrial revolution.

CHAPTER OBJECTIVES

After studying this chapter you should be able to:

√ identify the central concepts of transformational and transactional leadership,

√ understand the factors comprising transformational and transactional leadership,

√ detail the assumptions of organizational culture,

√ identify the relevant elements of organizational culture, and

√ understand the implications of symbolic leadership.

INTRODUCTION

In the 1960s and 1970s, disillusionment with the promises of scientific progress and the Enlightenment may have contributed to a shift away from scientific approaches to leadership. Transformational, cultural, and symbolic theories move away from thinking about discrete, measurable elements and define leadership in the rather unscientific terms of morality, values, meaning, and identity. Transformational theory is particularly concerned with ethics, and the moral character of leaders, followers, and their endeavors. Cultural leadership understands leaders in terms of their central role as models or creators of group culture. That culture, in turn, is primarily a product and expression of certain core values. Symbolic leadership, with a slightly different emphasis, sees leaders as the primary architects and representatives of meaning for the group and its members.

TRANSFORMATIONAL LEADERSHIP THEORY

The original formulation of transformational (transforming) leadership theory comes from the work of James MacGregor Burns in his Pulitzer Prize winning 1978 book, *Leadership*. At the core of transformational leadership is the concept of transformation of the both followers and leaders (Barge, 1994; Bennis & Nanus, 1985; Yukl, 1989). Tichy and Devanna (1986) suggest that transformational leaders are unique people who have the ability to impact, change, or discard the status quo.

The change they are being asked to make is not marginal; it is fundamental. It demands the commitment of the many, not the few. Its nature is revolutionary not evolutionary. It cries out for leaders, not managers.

Tichy & Devanna (1986)

Burns defined transformational leadership as a process in which "leaders and followers raise one another to higher levels of morality and motivation" (p. 20). A chief element of transformation, in Burns's view, centers around the ability to address the real needs of followers. Effective leadership is predicated on the assumption that advancing people up Maslow's hierarchy of needs is a necessary objective. Morality, to Burns, is the central measure of transformation. Values serve as a leader's guideposts. Transforming leaders are driven by values and moral principles that transcend the normal bartering or exchange mentality of *transactional* leadership.

Burns contrasted transforming leadership with "transactional leadership," a kind of leadership that takes place when one person initiates contact with another for the purpose of exchanging items of value. The exchange could be economic, political, or even psychological, as when one person exchanges hospitality in return for companionship. Power resources are important in the transaction, and the purposes involved are self-centered rather than truly mutual. The "bargainers" are not bound together beyond the exchange by any sort of higher purpose.

According to Burns, transformational leadership is distinguished by its focus on needs, which makes it accountable to the source of leadership - the follower. Two needs in particular emerge from a reading of Burns. First, Burns contended that people are driven by a moral need, something close to the core of humanity and human motivation. Burns associated this drive with the need to champion a cause, or the need to take a higher moral stance on an issue. The second need centers around paradoxical drives for consistency and conflict. Burns wrote, "Conflict - disagreement over goals within an array of followers, fear of outsiders, competition for scarce resources - immensely invigorates the mobilization of consensus and dissensus" (p. 40). Transforming leaders, according to Burns, help followers make sense of inconsistency to arrive at a satisfactory solution.

Burns offered the following specific characteristics of transforming leadership:

- *Transformational leadership is collective rather than focused on the leader personally.* Needs beyond the growth of a leader's power must be pursued.

- *Transformational leadership is dissensual and promotes change as a rule rather than simple status quo inaction.* Change emerges from conflict; consensus and consistency from dissensus.

- *Transformational leadership is causative rather than reactive or inactive.* The central component, the creation of change, emerges from the transformation of values and morality rather than reinforcement of transactional norms.

- *Transformational leadership is morally purposeful.* The ability to raise followers to a higher moral plane serves to motivate and renew, rather than reinforce transactional habits.

- *Transformational leadership is elevating.* Transformation means that followers must move to a higher level; there must be challenge and growth. This growth, according to Burns, must be moral growth centered around personal and collective values.

The process of transformation is empathetic, understanding, insightful, and considerate; the process of transformation is not manipulation, power-wielding, or coercion.
Burns (1978)

Bass (1985) claimed that transactional leadership (based on exchange, and designed to gain and manage resources) and transformational leadership, rather than being definitional opposites, were more similar than Burns had suggested. Bass reasoned that transactional leadership can have positive effects, and that transformational leadership could grow from it. Bass (1985, 1990) acknowledged that transformational leadership was superior to transactional, and modified Burns's description somewhat by adding some elements. Bass (1990) sees transformational leadership as:

- charismatic,
- inspirational,
- individually considerate, and
- intellectually stimulating.

Transactional leaders, on the other hand, are characterized by:

- the use of contingent rewards
- active and passive management by exception

Bass (1990) reasoned that a move toward transformational leadership would make companies more productive and ultimately more economically, socially, and interpersonally successful.

He feels strongly that the presence of transformational leadership will make companies more productive and ultimately more economically, socially, and interpersonally successful.

Yukl (1989) noted that transformational leadership is, at its core, a process utilizing micro-level and macro-level influences. At the macro-level, transformational leaders must be able to take charge of the social systems and reform the organization by creating an appropriate power situation. At the micro-level, transformational leaders must pay particular attention to the personalities in the organization to facilitate change at an interpersonal level. Tichy and Devanna (1986) went to great lengths to explain the process of transformation. They conclude that transformational leaders begin with a social fabric, then disrupt that environment and recreate the social fabric in a manner that better suits the needs and purposes of the group.

Barker (1994) argued that transforming leadership is based on interaction and influence rather than on directive power acts. He saw leadership as a non-linear social process that is constrained by an ethic and emerges from a crisis. Transformational leaders, he suggested, are interested in collective results rather than individual gain. Barker believed that transformational leadership goes beyond increases in productivity and performance, as advocated in traditional leadership theories, and embraces a theory of change centered around human potential and the common good.

Transformational leadership offered a radical alternative to theories centered on traits, styles, behaviors, and situations. It opened the door to a paradigmatic shift in conceptions of leadership from industrial to post-industrial. Other research centering on culture, symbols, and the values and meaning in which they are rooted soon followed.

ORGANIZATIONAL CULTURE AND LEADERSHIP

As transformational leadership began to attract attention, a related theory made its debut – the leader as creator of organizational culture. This theory has its origins in Terrence Deal and Allen Kennedy's 1982 book, *Corporate Cultures*. Deal and Kennedy developed their thinking around a few assumptions relative to organizations:

- *Every organization has a culture.* A culture is the way that companies do their business, or "the way we do things around here" (p. 4).

- *Strong cultures mean success for their members.* They asserted that "a strong culture has almost always been the driving force behind continuing success in American business" (p. 5).

- *Culture is symbolic and manageable.* The culture of an organization can be recast whenever the need arises by changing any significant factor of organizational life.

- *Any organization has core values that dictate the rest of the culture.* Values comprise the bedrock of corporate culture and must be seen as the foundational elements when building or rebuilding a corporate culture.

- *Organizational culture can be affected by change.* Changes in the culture will follow if the people, heroes, rituals/ceremonies, or communication style of an organization is altered.

Leadership and organizational culture are inextricably linked and depend on each other for organizational success.

During this same period, Peters and Waterman (1982) were studying modern organizations and finding that successful organizations were those that had clear values, knew their market, and could adapt their organization without selling out their values. Peters and Waterman identified these important characteristics through their study of organizations that had been identified as the "success stories" of their day.

Schein (1992) argued that leadership and organizational culture are interdependent, so organizations must have both to succeed. Several elements and patterns emerge from Schein's research. Each element plays an important symbolic role, and allows the culture to reveal itself to participants in a "public" manner. Some of these symbolic elements—artifacts, rites, rituals, or heroes—are highly visible, central fixtures of organizational life. Members of the organizational culture, however, have some latitude in interpreting and responding to these elements.

The following table outlines Schein's symbolic elements and their manifestations in organizational culture.

Elements of Organizational Culture

Element	Description
Values are:	- The bedrock of corporate culture and identify the organization - Fixed, stable; difficult to adapt or manage; known by all - Difficult to measure and assess, somewhat subjective - Communicated in stories, rites and rituals, in corporate communications, and by heroes - Made explicit in mission statements, value statements, and internal or external documents
Symbols are:	- The "language" spoken in the organization - Shared, as a common code is essential for meaning - Learned from being around other members of the culture - Can exclude those not members of the culture - Used in internal and external organizational statements, speeches, conversations, training, and meetings
Rites and Rituals are:	- Special events that dramatize the values of the organization - Common and habitual modes of behavior, such as coffee breaks, lunch breaks, meeting behavior, customary attire - Special events that symbolize cultural values for the internal public, such as 20-year awards, recognition for special achievement, holiday parties, etc - Celebrations that display the culture to the external public, such as inaugural balls, company banquets, et
Heroes are:	- People who personify organizational values - Founders whose vision shaped organizational identity - CEOs, officers, and high-status people who formally represent the company - Mavericks or risk agents who change the organizational landscape - Persons such as Microsoft's Bill Gates or Ford Motor Company's Henry Ford
Stories:	- Demonstrate examples of success or failure relative to the values of the organization - Need not be true, just believable - Are often heard and repeated through the organizational grapevine - Exalt appropriate or admirable behavior
Artifacts:	- Are the embodiment of cultural values - Find their meaning in the central tenets of the culture - Are usually numerous, found everywhere in the organization but are unique to it - Can include special awards, special or ordinary machines, or corporate trophies

SYMBOLIC LEADERSHIP

Symbolic leadership emphasizes the role of the leader in defining or representing organizational identity and purpose. Bennis and Nanus (1985) suggested that leaders are the ultimate creators of organizational meaning. They are, in effect, the "social architects" of organizations. Hackman and Johnson (1996) suggest that effective leaders are those who have learned to master the symbolic realm. All organizational members spin webs of meaning based on the information they receive. The role of the social/symbolic architect is to communicate clearly and dynamically the information and ideas that will help members spin those webs in a manner consistent with organizational values and beliefs. Leaders are seen as the primary, most powerful agents for providing meaning, developing commitment, and institutionalizing an organizational vision.

Symbolic leadership theory focuses heavily on communication, but goes well beyond the 1940s leader communicator styles identified by Lewin, Lippitt, and White. As discussed in Chapter 4, these early researchers concluded that leaders communicate in a manner consistent with their particular style of leadership (autocratic, democratic, or laissez-faire), but did not recognize the symbolic function of leader communication.

One of the main differences between leadership and management centers on this issue of effectively symbolizing the organization.

Bennis & Nanus (1985)

Symbolic leadership theorists are particularly interested in the role of the leader in creating a clear and compelling vision for organizations. Bennis and Nanus posit that clear vision enables an organization to build the values that strengthen culture. Leadership is an art that involves organizing, interpreting, and selling such a vision. Above all else, a symbolic leader must be a skilled communicator to be effective. Symbolic leaders use influence rather than power to communicate and instill vision, and so must have at their disposal a fully-developed symbolic repertoire (Bennis & Nanus, 1985; Sypher, 1990).

Symbolic leadership theorists make very specific arguments regarding the difference between leadership and management. They see leaders function as the highly visible, social/symbolic architects, while managers perform the day-in and day-out, routine activities of "running the business." Leaders are substantially different from managers in that the symbolic role of the former is more subjective and idealized, while the latter plays a more objective, pragmatic, functional role.

SUMMARY

Transformational, cultural, and symbolic leadership theories offer new answers to old questions about leadership. Transformational theory clarifies important differences between change rooted in moral ideals and managerial transactions rooted in cost/benefit analyses. Cultural theory provides new insights linking organizational success to strong organizational culture and values. Symbolic theory recognizes the importance of the leader as a visible symbol, particularly in information-rich environments where image is critical.

REFERENCES

Barge, J. K. (1994). *Leadership: Communication skills for organizations and groups.* New York: St. Martin's.

Barker, R. A. (1994). "The rethinking of leadership." *Journal of Leadership Studies,* 1 (2), 46-54.

Bass, B. M. (1985*). Leadership and performance beyond expectations.* New York: Free Press.

Bass, B. M. (1990). *Bass and Stogdill's handbook of leadership: Theory, research, and managerial application* (3rd edition). New York: Free Press.

Bennis, W. & Nanus, B. (1985). *Leaders: The strategies for taking charge.* New York: Harper & Row.

Burns, J. M. (1978). *Leadership.* Free Press: New York.

Deal, T. E. & Kennedy, A. A. (1982). Corporate cultures. Reading, MA: Addison Wesley.

Egan, R. F., Sarros, J. C., & Santora, J. C. (1995). "Putting transactional and transformational leadership into practice." *Journal of Leadership Studies,* 2 (3), 100-123.

Hackman, M. Z. & Johnson, C. E. (1996). *Leadership: A communication perspective* (2nd ed.). Prospect Heights, IL: Waveland.

Peters, T. J., & Waterman, R. H. (1982). *In search of excellence.* New York: Harper and Row.

Potts, J. D. (2001). *The ethical difference: Why leaders are more than managers.* Longmont, CO: Rocky Mountain Press.

Schein, E. H. (1992). *Organizational culture and leadership* (2nd ed.). San Francisco, CA: Jossey-Bass.

Sypher, B. D. (1990). A message centered approach to the study of leadership. In J. A. Anderson (Ed.) *Communication Yearbook 14.* Newbury Park, CA: Sage.

Chapter 7

Name _____

DISCUSSION QUESTIONS

1. Discuss your thoughts on the difference between transformational and transactional leadership. Give examples of how each might be important to an organization.

_____

_____

_____

_____

_____

_____

_____

_____

2. What is the difference between a strong and a weak organizational culture? Give specific examples to illustrate the differences.

_____

_____

_____

_____

_____

_____

_____

_____

3. Imagine yourself as the leader of an organization. List 4 or 5 specific actions you will take to be effective as a symbolic leader.

_____

_____

_____

_____

_____

_____

_____

_____

_____

_____

_____

_____

_____

_____

_____

_____

_____

_____

_____

Chapter 7

ACTIVITY

To better understand the nature of organizational culture, try this exercise. It will take about 2 hours to complete. First, take 1 hour to visit an organization. Without interfering, observe how people interact with one another. Look for heroes or artifacts and note the special symbols/language used. During your observation jot down a few notes, but concentrate more on observing. When you are finished observing, complete the following chart:

Artifacts	
Symbols and Language	
Heroes	
Values	

1. Summarize the culture based on your limited observation.

_____

_____

_____

_____

_____

_____

_____

_____

_____

_____

_____

_____

_____

_____

_____

_____

_____

_____

_____

CONTEMPORARY
LEADERSHIP

Though leadership theories developed over the past century have provided a wealth of information and insight, many of their fundamental working assumptions are no longer accepted. Theories of leadership have had to adapt to see changes in society with the passing of the industrial age and the dawning of a new world driven by information and knowledge. This unit explores a profound change—a paradigm shift—in the way leadership is viewed, and introduces several contemporary theories that have sprung from this new perspective.

CHAPTER 8

THE NEW AGE OF LEADERSHIP

*This chapter describes a paradigm shift in the study of leadership, a shift rooted in a new and fundamental distinction between the development of leaders and the development of leadership. The characteristics of the post-industrial view of **leadership** are contrasted with traditional approaches to **leading**. A new definition of leadership is presented, and contemporary models centering on shared leadership are discussed.*

CHAPTER OBJECTIVES

After studying this chapter you should be able to:
- √ describe the dramatic shift in the study of leadership,
- √ list and explain the key components of contemporary definitions of leadership,
- √ explain the distinction between leadership development and leader development,
- √ summarize the difference between the industrial view and the post-industrial (contemporary) view of leadership, and
- √ explain why collaborative relationships are at the core of today's distributed leadership process.

INTRODUCTION

In the late 1980s and early 1990s, a small group of innovative scholars began to talk and write about a new age in the understanding of leadership. They believed that a view radically different from previous approaches was needed to accurately depict the organizational and social landscape. Most of this chapter focuses on the work of Joseph Rost of the University of San Diego. Rost is widely known for his recognition and description of the shift from the industrial to what he refers to as the "post-industrial" model of leadership. Rost's new definition of leadership in the post-industrial era has had a major impact on the field of leadership studies.

A NEW DEFINITION

The desire to define and explain the essence of leadership has interested researchers and scholars for nearly a century. Up until recently, conceptions of leadership focused on a single person and his or her personal qualities or skills. Using the techniques of social science, researchers tried to identify what abilities, traits, behaviors, types of power, or aspects of situations could be isolated and used in determining how effective a leader would be.

The birth and evolution of the contemporary idea of leader**ship** focuses on a much more complex concept that includes more than the individual leader. Recent definitions reject the idea that leadership revolves around the leader's actions, abilities, behaviors, styles, or charisma. Scholars now understand the basic nature of leadership in terms of the *interaction* among the people involved in the process—in terms of what leaders and followers do together. Leadership is now not seen as the activity of a single person. Rather, it is explained and defined as a *collaborative endeavor* among group members. The essence of leadership, therefore, does not have to do with the leader, but with the relationship.

*The birth and evolution of the idea of 'leader**ship**" focuses on a much more complex concept that reaches beyond the individual leader.*

One result of this transformation in the concept of leadership has been the reconstruction of leadership definitions. In his ground-breaking book, *Leadership for the Twenty-First Century* (1991), Joseph Rost articulates a definition of leadership based on this post-industrial perspective, a definition he believes is more consistent with contemporary organizational life. Rost's definition says that "*leadership is an influence relationship among leaders and followers who intend real changes that reflect their mutual purposes.*"

This definition is composed of four basic components, each of which is essential and must be present if a particular relationship is to be called leadership.

> *"Leadership is an influence relationship among leaders and followers who intend real changes that reflect their mutual purposes."*
> (Rost, 1991)

- *The relationship is based on influence.* This influence is multi-directional, meaning that influence is multi-directional (not just top-down), and the influence attempts must not be coercive. Therefore, the relationship is not based on authority, but rather persuasion.

- *Leaders and followers are the people in this relationship.* If leadership is defined as a relationship, then both leaders and followers are practicing leadership. Rost does not say that all players in the relationship are equal, but he does say all active players practice influence. Typically, there is more than one follower and more than one leader in the relationship.

- *Leaders and followers intend real changes.* "Intend" means that the leaders and followers promote and purposefully seek change. "Real" means that changes intended by leaders and followers are substantial.

- *The changes the leaders and followers intend reflect their mutual purposes.* The key is that, in a leadership relationship, desired changes not only reflect the desires of the leader, but also the desires of the followers.

LEADERSHIP VS. LEADER DEVELOPMENT

Under the industrial paradigm, training leaders was of primary importance. People who were thrust into management roles often needed training to help them succeed as leaders. With the shift to the post-industrial paradigm, more focus is being put on *leadership* development. Until recently, "leader development programs" and "leadership development programs" were synonymous. But under the post-industrial paradigm, there is a difference, and that difference is critical.

Rost (1993) contends that scholars, trainers, developers, and practitioners "must rethink their old assumptions about leader development." Leader development programs— those seminars, programs, and workshops that focus on developing the leader rather than the relationship between leaders and followers—are still popular. In fact, numerous colleges and universities still accept this traditional approach. Programs that recognize leadership and focus on leadership as relationship, however, invest time and effort in developing skills, attitudes, and behaviors that will foster more collaborative relationships. The emphasis is no longer simply on teaching leaders to play the role of leaders.

The concept of shared leadership, addressed later in this chapter, requires both leaders and followers to play an active role in the leadership process. If contemporary theories are correct, leader development alone is not the formula for success in the twenty-first century.

THE POST-INDUSTRIAL VIEW

Recent developments in views of leadership reflect similar shift in other disciplines away from descriptions of the world as objective, linear, single, mechanical, hierarchic, and controllable. The post-industrial view of leadership emphasizes collaboration, power-sharing, facilitation and empowerment. Similar to trends in other disciplines, this reflects a new view of the world as a complex, diverse, interactive and dynamic environment.

Leadership is more about a relationship than an individual.

This comparison shows that the emerging post-industrial view of leadership is quite different from the earlier approaches. Rost tells us that:

- Leadership is more about a relationship than an individual.
- The leadership process is distinct and different than management.
- Leadership focuses on the interaction of leaders and follows not just the behavior of leaders.
- Leadership seeks mutual purposes rather than the leader's wishes.
- Leadership desires deep and real changes.
- Influence tactics are the only acceptable behaviors.
- The leadership process is something that is not done all the time.

In many ways, leadership under the industrial paradigm was nearly impossible to distinguish from management. But Rost and other contemporary theorists insist that leadership can in no way be equated with management. The contrast between the two is outlined in the chart on the following page.

	INDUSTRIAL PARADIGM	POST-INDUSTRIAL PARADIGM
Rost's Paradigm Contrast Chart	- Individual	- Relationship
	- Good management	- Process distinctly different from management
	- Leader behaviors/traits	- Leaders and collaborators interacting in a relationship
	- Do what the leader wishes	- Do what both leaders and collaborators wish
	- Pursue any and all organizational goals	- Pursue mutual purposes that intend real changes
	- Use any means	- Use influence behaviors only
	- Practiced continuously	- Practiced episodically
	- Safe	- Risk-taking
	- Control	- Freedom
	- Stability	- Change and movement
	- Hierarchical	- Non-hierarchical
	- Weak followers	- Strong followers
	- Coercive influence	- Non-coercive influence
	- Directive style	- Collaborative approach
	- Top-down	- Empowerment
	- Results-oriented	- Process-oriented

One of the most notable themes in contemporary theory has to do with the role of followers. The 75-year history of the industrial perspective places almost no emphasis on the important role followers play in the leadership process. It was assumed that followers were unimportant because leadership was no more than what leaders wanted and did. Followers did not really count in leader-centered views of leadership. Post-industrial theories, on the other hand, put followers on equal footing with leaders in the leadership process. If we define leadership as a relationship, then we must recognize the contributions of those who collaborate with leaders.

Leadership is not what leaders do. Rather, leadership is what leaders and followers do together to accomplish their mutual purposes. Leaders in today's society interact with followers in a shared-power environment. Individual leaders no longer have all of the information and power needed to make substantial changes. In modern society, many people participate in leadership, some as leaders and others as followers.

DISTRIBUTED LEADERSHIP

Leadership is not what leaders do. Leadership is what leaders and followers do together to accomplish their mutual purposes.

The post-industrial consideration given to the activities of followers contrasts sharply with the industrial paradigm's passive view of followers. Followers were seen as a necessary evil that had to be managed and controlled. The contribution of followers was both simple and troublesome—they were chaotic variables that could interfere with the structure leaders attempted to impose.

Contemporary theorists see followers not only as major players in organizations, but also as the major reason organizations succeed. Studies of Japanese organizations have shown that "workers" (a.k.a., followers) contribute more to the success of their firms than does management. Deming showed that quality started on the line and went all the way to the top.

Movement away from the industrial paradigm has to do with followers in another sense. Under the old system, people at lower levels had little input regarding the functioning of their organization. Followers were easily mistreated and generally under-appreciated. As these important individuals began to recognize their value, and what they could contribute, self-motivated teams took it upon themselves to speak up, to contribute, and to intervene in saving their companies rather than looking to "heroic" leaders to handle problems (Yukl, 1998). Leadership researchers sensed this discontent during the 1970s, and began to develop the concept of distributed, or shared leadership.

Shared leadership looks to the appointed leader to give all members the opportunity to exercise expertise as appropriate situations arise. Viewing leaders and followers as equal partners in the process is the centerpiece of shared leadership, for it depends on both the willingness of the leader and the competency of the follower (Gardner, 1990). Yukl (1998) believes that shared leadership, though new, is quickly spreading. More work is being done in the areas of self-managed teams, cooperatives, and employee-managed workplaces.

SUMMARY

What many theorists see as a "new age" of leadership is characterized by a fundamental shift in the way people view, study, and practice leadership. Today's approaches have little in common with older assumptions that autocratic leaders should control events. Instead, contemporary models talk of leaders and followers participating together in the process called leadership. That process involves both leaders and collaborators working *together* to bring about meaningful change for the good of all parties. The chapters that follow outline several contemporary theories shaped by the post-industrial paradigm.

REFERENCES

Bennis, W. & Nanus, B. (1985). *Leaders: The strategies for taking charge.* New York: Harper & Row.

Brungardt, C.L., Gould, L.V., Potts, J., and Moore, R. (1997). "The emergence of leadership studies: Linking the traditional outcomes of liberal education with leadership development." *The Journal of Leadership Studies* (4).

Brungardt, C.L. (1998). "The new face of leadership: Implications for training educational leaders." *On the Horizon* (7).

Chrislip, D.D., and Larson, C.E. (1994). *Collaborative leadership: How citizens and civic leaders can make a difference.* San Francisco: Jossey-Bass.

Gardner, J. (1990). *On leadership.* New York: Free Press.

Rogers, J. L. "Leadership Development for the '90s: Incorporating Emergent Paradigm Perspectives." *NASPA Journal,* Summer 1992.

Rosenbach, W.E., and Taylor, R.L. (Eds.) (1989). *Contemporary Issues in Leadership* (2nd Edition). Boulder, CO: Westview Press.

Rost, J. C. (1991). *Leadership in the twenty-first century.* New York: Praeger.

Rost, J. C. (1993). "Leadership Development in the New Millennium." *Journal of Leadership Studies* (1).

Rost, J.C. (1997). "Moving from Industrial to Relationship: A Post-industrial Paradigm of Leadership." *Journal of Leadership Studies* (4).

Wren, J.T. (1995). *The leader's companion: Insights on leadership through the ages.* New York: Free Press.

Yukl, G. (1998). *Leadership in organizations* (4th ed.). New York: Prentice Hall.

Chapter 8 **Name** _____

DISCUSSION QUESTIONS

1. What is the essence of the *industrial view* of leadership?

_____

_____

_____

_____

_____

_____

2. What is the essence of the *post-industrial view* of leadership?

_____

_____

_____

_____

_____

_____

_____

3. Compare a specific post-industrial leader to a specific industrial leader.

_____

_____

_____

_____

_____

_____

4. Describe the important components of Rost's definition.

_____

_____

_____

_____

_____

_____

_____

_____

_____

5. How is the role of followers different under the post-industrial view of leadership?

_____

_____

_____

_____

_____

_____

_____

_____

_____

Name _____

CASE STUDY

In the following case study, try to imagine what the people involved are thinking. Also, identify the behaviors that are occurring. Then develop your answers to the questions that follow.

Professor Susan Jorgensen had been the motive force behind the newest undergraduate major on the City University campus: Women and Cultural Studies. Dr. Jorgensen was brought in 5 years ago to design, develop, and implement the new major at CU. She was given a nice budget that allowed her to hire three new faculty, operating expenses above the standard for other departments, and a large scholarship fund to help recruit the best and brightest students to the new major. Everything was great until the end of the recent fall semester.

During the last week of class, one of the new faculty members, Dr. Kevin Parks, put himself in a difficult situation when he changed the requirements of a course and added an additional final oral examination to be taken individually by each student. Professor Jorgensen had heard rumors that Dr. Parks was known for challenging students in unconventional ways, and sometimes even publicly ridiculing them. Dr. Parks had favorite students in the class, as well as students to whom he did not respond well. He even admitted this in his first tenure hearing.

What Professor Jorgensen did not know was that Parks was failing nearly 40% of the class and hoped to use the final exam as a "nail in their coffin" so that they could later be dismissed from the program. The class that Parks taught was a gateway class – students needed passing marks in the class in order to continue in the new major.

As she became aware of this situation, Dr. Jorgensen informed the Dean of City University of the issues. The Dean, Dr. Mike Stafford, was quite managerial in his approach to problem solving, and generally said "either make the faculty work for you, or get rid of them". On other occasions, he had warned Dr. Jorgensen that if she could not get her faculty to work harder, he would "find another person who could do it better". Dean Stafford was a retired Marine, and liked the programs under his supervision to have strict parameters and clear objectives. This case was no different, except the stakes were higher and the tolerance for Dr. Parks' antics had grown very slim at the Dean's level. Dr. Jorgensen's leadership style, alternatively, was much more participative and open. Susan liked to gather input from the parties involved and make decisions via consensus. She had always sought to improve the department by coaching and collaborating, rather than by controlling and coercing.

Considering these factors, please answer the following questions.

1. What are Dr. Jorgensen's options regarding Dr. Parks and his class? List the possible solutions to the problem.

_____

_____

_____

_____

_____

2. For each solution, provide a brief analysis of whether it is an industrial or post-industrial approach. Explain your choices.

_____

_____

_____

_____

_____

_____

3. Which option(s) would most impress Dean Stafford? Which option(s) might cause Dean Stafford to further question Dr. Jorgensen's abilities?

_____

_____

_____

_____

_____

_____

_____

_____

SOCIAL CHANGE LEADERSHIP

In this chapter, a contemporary theory called social change leadership is discussed. This understanding of leadership focuses on the concepts of change, collaboration, and civic responsibility. Social change leadership encourages the development of citizen leaders who will pursue community change that benefits the common good.

CHAPTER OBJECTIVES

After studying this chapter you should be able to:

√ identify the characteristics of a citizen leader,

√ understand the basic components that comprise the social change leadership theory,

√ recognize the importance that collaboration plays in collective action,

√ understand the UCLA model of social change leadership, and

√ recognize that the purpose of social change leadership is to address and solve social problems.

INTRODUCTION

It is often said today that too few are willing to stand up and address the truly serious problems facing society—that too many people are uninterested in making a difference in their own communities. Interestingly, societal indicators show that as social problems increase, public activism decreases. Many argue, therefore, that we must intentionally encourage and motivate ourselves and our fellow citizens to develop skills and commit energy to activities that benefit society.

> *Social change leadership is a call for each of us to serve as citizen leaders.*

Social change leadership theory seeks to develop "social change agents" who will address and solve community problems. This model of leadership emphasizes collective action through collaboration for the purpose of addressing social needs and injustices. It is a contemporary theory that calls for the development of citizen leaders committed to making the world a better place. In its simplest form, social change leadership encourages us to be responsible both for ourselves and for those around us. Social change theory starts with the basic assumption that all persons have the ability to lead, and therefore should participate in civic action for the purpose of making a difference in our communities.

This chapter reviews three variations of social change leadership. First, developed in the early 1990s by a group of faculty members at Fort Hays State University, *social change leadership theory* is presented. Next, Chrislip and Larson's *collaborative leadership* model is discussed. Finally, the 7 C's of UCLA's *social change model of leadership development* is explored.

SOCIAL CHANGE LEADERSHIP THEORY

In the spring of 1993, a curriculum development committee at Fort Hays State University developed and then implemented a comprehensive academic leadership studies program based on a social change model. This curriculum focused on the "what, how, and why" of leadership. These three organizing curricular elements were summarized respectively as creating change, collaboration, and civic leadership.

Conceptually defined, leadership is about *creating change*. Consistent with contemporary definitions, leadership is about making both personal and organizational changes. *Collaborative leadership* tells us we need new approaches to how we practice and participate in the leadership process. Finally, the *civic leadership* focus provides the meaning and sense of purpose behind leadership involvement.

Creating Change

First and foremost, leadership is about creating change. The concept of change is what makes leadership different from all other forms of human interaction. Leadership is a process of change wherein both leaders and followers alike serve as change agents. Thus, those actively involved in leadership are both subject to and the driving force behind change.

First and foremost, leadership is about creating change.

There are several other important elements within the theme of creating change. First, social change leadership involves "purposefully" seeking change that is intentionally designed and implemented by the change agents. Secondly, it involves transformational or fundamental change, rather than small incremental adjustments. In most cases, it is change that requires long-term commitment. Third, the purpose of change is positive movement. Therefore, leadership is about making improvements and correcting discrepancies between "what is" and "what ought to be" for all members of a community or society.

Collaboration

If leadership is about creating and encouraging useful change, then the next question has to do with how should those changes should be initiated and sustained. In social change theory, the answer is collaboration. This theory assumes that methods of practicing leadership must reflect a contemporary view of organizational life to be successful. Because that life is now characterized by cooperation, power sharing, and empowerment, successful teams today are those organizations or communities that manifest an ability to bring people together for collective action.

Civic Leadership

The third and final curricular theme focuses on the motivation for practicing and participating in leadership. If leadership is an influence relationship for change, and collaborative approaches are the preferred methods, then the final concern has to do with making sure that the changes pursued will result in improvements for society. Social change leadership argues that individuals must ask themselves and others to believe in something larger than personal self-interest as they become active players in the leadership process. The civic theme represents a shift in leadership from goal attainment for the *collective* good (the good of groups or organizations), to leadership that emphasizes the *common* good (the good of society as a whole). This theme encourages all persons to take action on behalf of this larger good. Very simply, each citizen has a responsibility to carry change forward.

COLLABORATIVE LEADERSHIP

Drawing on extensive research in community action and collaboration, Chrislip and Larson (1994) provide us with a social change approach that encourages citizens to become community leaders. *Collaborative Leadership* is designed to help bring together diverse community groups for the purpose of making real and measurable changes in their communities. This model for social change assumes that traditional community problem-solving efforts are inadequate. New collaborative efforts are needed to bring people together to successfully address complex public issues.

Ten Keys to Successful Collaboration

We must develop new collaborative efforts that bring people together to successfully address complex public issues.

Chrislip and Larson provide ten important elements or conditions that describe how to design, initiate, and sustain a collaborative social change process. These are steps that must be present or built into the collaborative process if attempts at social change are to succeed:

- *Good timing and clear need.* There must be a sense of urgency among stakeholders in order to provide the needed momentum for the effort.

- *Strong stakeholder groups.* The process must include stakeholder groups that are well organized and represent the variety of people from the community.

- *Broad-based involvement.* This process must also include participants from diverse sectors (government, business, etc.).

- *Credibility and openness of process.* It is critical that the collaborative process be seen as fair, open, and credible by all stakeholder groups.

- *Commitment* (at the individual level) is the ability to dedicate oneself to both the need for change and the actual path to change that is chosen.

- *Support or acquiescence of established authorities or powers.* Recognized authorities must agree not to undermine the results or recommendation of the process.

- *Overcoming mistrust and skepticism.* As the process moves forward, skepticism and mistrust must decrease if the process is to be successful.

- *Strong leadership in the process.* The collaborative process must include strong leadership that allows for and encourages fairness and openness rather than the point of view of one stakeholder group.
- *Interim success.* To keep participants motivated, community players must celebrate their successes along the way.
- *A shift to broader concerns.* Finally, the process must encourage participants to move from narrow interests to the broader concerns of the community.

Benefits of Collaboration

Chrislip and Larson's basic premise is unambiguously stated: "If you bring the appropriate people together in constructive ways with good information, they will create authentic visions and strategies for addressing the shared concerns of their organization..." (p. 14). Working together, they assert, is the key to truly effective leadership. Success is measured by useful change, as in when it moves organizations and communities to an improved position. They further reason that collaboration is powerful due to the benefits that can be achieved. They suggest that collaboration can:

Working together, Chrislip and Larson assert, is the key to truly effective leadership.

- *Achieve tangible results.* Results can be achieved when people work together with one focus. Working with other committed people often leads to a high degree of synergy, which produces uncommon results.
- *Institutionalize effective problem-solving processes.* Once some degree of success is gained from collaboration, it becomes the model of choice for solving problems that face the organization.
- *Empower both leaders and followers.* Often, one or two people become motivated about a project while others in the organization fail to share that motivation. Collaboration, properly enacted, helps to overcome such problems by motivating a broader cohort of leaders and followers.
- *Change the way that leaders and followers solve public and organizational problems.* When adopting a collaborative framework, leader and followers strive to solve problems by fully sharing information with all parties and being inclusive, not exclusive. Through ownership, creation of solutions involving all constituents takes on added importance.

THE UCLA LEADERSHIP MODEL

In 1996, Helen and Alexander Astin of the Higher Education Research Institute at UCLA published a guidebook entitled *A Social Change Model of Leadership Development*. This guidebook provides suggestions regarding how and why to encourage individuals to serve as social change agents in their communities. The report stresses citizen leadership, saying, "We believe that it is possible for all individuals to be leaders, to develop leadership skills, and to make a difference in society."

This model provides a framework for leadership development that is built on three levels of interaction, all revolving around the concept of change. First, the *individual level* focuses on the personal traits needed to produce social change. Secondly, the *group level* focuses on our ability to collaborate with our neighbors. Thirdly, the *community/society level* focuses on utilizing leadership for social concerns.

The 7 C's of Change

Within the three levels of interaction, the authors provide us with what they call the 7 C's of change. These are seven basic values or attributes needed to encourage or participate in positive social change movements. They include:

1. *Consciousness of self* (individual level) means to know one's self, including values, emotions, and attitudes. Before we can contribute to a larger effort, it is imperative that we understand ourselves.

2. *Congruence* (individual level) is motivation needed to provide the energy and passion to drive the change effort.

3. *Commitment* (individual level) is the ability to dedicate oneself to change and to a specific path for pursuing change.

4. *Collaboration* (group level) stresses the importance of working together to positively address complex societal issues.

5. *Common purpose* (group level) suggests that all active participants must share some basic values and goals if the collaborative effort is to succeed.

6. *Controversy with civility* (group level) means that during any group effort, differences will emerge, but the diversity of viewpoints must be addressed through open and honest discussion.

7. *Citizenship* (community level) implies that the purpose of both individual and group activities is service to the community.

> "We believe that it is possible for all individuals to be leaders, to develop leadership skills, and to make a difference in society."

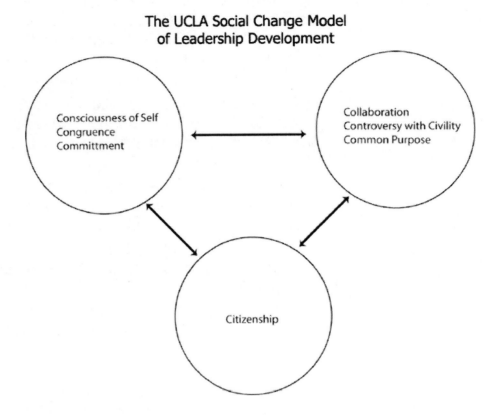

The UCLA Social Change Model
of Leadership Development

SUMMARY

Social change leadership is a contemporary approach to the study and practice of leadership. The *social change leadership theory, collaborative leadership*, and the *social change model of leadership development* are all examples of efforts to develop and encourage citizen leaders to address community problems. This approach to leadership embraces collaborative methods as the way to initiate and sustain positive action. Finally, social change leadership is a call for all of individuals to assume roles as social change agents in an effort to make the world a better place.

REFERENCES

Astin, A.W. & Scherrei, R.A. (1980). *Maximizing leadership effectiveness*. San Francisco: Jossey-Bass.

Block, P. (1993). *Stewardship: Choosing service over self-interest*. San Francisco: Berrett-Koehler.

Brungardt, C.L., Gould, L.V., Potts, J., Moore, R. "The Emergence of Leadership Studies: Linking the Traditional Outcomes of Liberal Education with Leadership Development," *Journal of Leadership Studies*, Summer 1997, Vol. 4, No. 3.

Brungardt, C.L. (1999). *Social change leadership inventory: Self-assessment and analysis (2nd Edition)*. Longmont, CO: Rocky Mountain Institute for Leadership Advancement.

Bryson, J.M. & Crosby, B.C. (1992). *Leadership for the common good*. San Francisco: Jossey-Bass.

Chrislip, D.D., and Larson, C.E. (1994). *Collaborative leadership: How citizens and civic leaders can make a difference*. San Francisco: Jossey-Bass. Haas, H.G. (with Tamarkin, B.). (1992). *The leader within*. New York: Harper Collins.

Higher Education Research Institute, UCLA. (1996). *A social change model for leadership development*. Los Angeles: Higher Education Research Institute, UCLA.

Lappe, F.M. & DuBois, P.M. (1994). *The quickening of America: Rebuilding our nation, Remaking our lives*. San Francisco: Jossey-Bass.

Matusak, L.R. (1997). *Finding your voice: Learning to lean... Anywhere you want to make a difference*. San Francisco: Jossey-Bass.

McKenna, G., and Feingold, S. (1997). *Taking sides: Clashing views on controversial political issues* (10th ed.). New York: Dushkin Publishing Group, Inc.

Chapter 9   **Name** _____

DISCUSSION QUESTIONS

1. Describe the characteristics of a citizen leader.

_____

_____

_____

_____

_____

_____

_____

_____

_____

2. Discuss in detail the similarities of the 3 leadership models of social change presented in this chapter.

_____

_____

_____

_____

_____

_____

_____

_____

3. Discuss in detail the 3 components of the social change
leadership theory.

a. Creating Change _____

_____

_____

_____

_____

_____

_____

b. Collaboration _____

_____

_____

_____

_____

_____

_____

_____

c. Civic Leadership _____

_____

_____

_____

_____

_____

_____

_____

4. Discuss the 3 levels of interaction described in the social change model.

a. Individual level _____

_____

_____

_____

_____

b. Group level _____

_____

_____

_____

_____

c. Community/society level _____

_____

_____

_____

_____

4. What do you believe is the overall purpose of the social change approach to leadership? Explain.

_____

_____

_____

_____

_____

Chapter 9   **Name** _____

ACTIVITY

1. Provide an example of a social change leadership process that you have observed in your own community.

_____

_____

_____

_____

_____

_____

_____

_____

_____

2. If you decide to participate as a social change agent, what public issue or issues do you believe warrant immediate attention? What role could you play in the solution?

_____

_____

_____

_____

_____

_____

_____

_____

RISK LEADERSHIP

Risk leadership offers lower and middle level employees the chance to make real, lasting changes in their organization from the bottom up. Risk agents and the entire organization benefit when members at lower levels are willing to undertake risk leadership. The risk leadership process involves confronting and challenging the status quo, then working toward collaborative arrangements to address issues, resolve people problems, and stimulate genuine organizational transformation.

CHAPTER OBJECTIVES

After studying this chapter you should be able to:
√ understand and identify classical and progressive leadership,
√ explain the three forces that compel risk leaders to act,
√ understand and elaborate on risk leadership, risk agents, and the risk agency,
√ explain the risk leadership process,
√ list the outcomes of risk leadership, and
√ compare classical, progressive, and risk leadership models.

INTRODUCTION

Risk leadership encourages lower-level employees to confront and challenge authority as a means of transforming their organizations.

Risk leadership proposes a substantially different approach to organizational change and improvement. It assumes that there are times when classical and progressive leadership approaches are inadequate for creating the type of power arrangements needed to stimulate organizational growth. Risk leadership identifies *risk agents* who are motivated to initiate and sustain internal dissent because of organizational problems, failures on the part of top management, or failure on the part of the organization as a whole to respond to challenges.

Risk agents innovatively develop a *coalition of revolutionaries*—a *risk agency*—who empower themselves and alter power arrangements within the organizational structure. Through a series of revolutionary processes, the risk agency first challenges and then collaborates with management with the aim of moving the organization forward. Finally, risk leadership calls upon all members of an organization to recognize the value of this unique approach and encourage the development of a permanent culture that allows for healthy confrontation as a product of bottom-up empowerment.

ANTECEDENTS OF RISK LEADERSHIP

Perhaps the most common reason why any change happens is because it was a good idea at the time. *Issue-driven* revolt centers around one or more business *events* that illuminate building tension and frustration relative to poor business practices. When traditional business practices become outdated and ineffective, issue-driven revolt is frequently a viable option. Revolt based on a specific issue usually involves short-term commitment on the part of the risk agency for one specific problem. If it extends beyond that issue to a broader indictment of the organization, a qualitatively different kind of change—*transformative* change—is involved. Transformative change will be discussed in a moment.

It is important to note that *issue-driven* revolt challenges ideas, purposes, values, goals, and processes related to a *particular* issue or policy. Issue-driven revolt is not a product of division between people, but rather is forced by differences in people's ideas or positions. This does not mean that issue-driven revolt does not involve people taking sides, for the different sides of issues always have advocates. But issue-driven revolt always springs from a belief that the organization could be made better by improving a basic process, by changing a particular policy, by modifying certain values or mission statements, or by rethinking a fundamental organizational assumption.

Person-driven revolt is the next category of change defined by risk leadership. It recognizes the *power of one* in a negative sense: the negative actions of one person may be sufficient to spark a risk agency. Person-driven revolt happens when one person or a group of people, most often executives or top managers, unintentionally stimulate those who lack formal power to take action. When classical leadership becomes too oppressive—when so much control exists at the top that differences between people (as opposed to issues) dominate thinking—confrontation and challenges to that power are imminent. Person-driven revolt is divisive, personal, and invasive. It becomes a possibility when there is an extreme loss of faith in the leader or when a leader uses power unethically.

Person-driven revolt type of revolt also happens when there is sufficient belief that a leader is not competent enough to make the right decisions and choices (Hornstein, 1996). The basic point here is that not all conflict is based on issues. Personal differences may be so great between groups in an organization that revolt is the only way to control the controllers. Many personal differences can arise between risk agents and top management (Hornstein, 1996), simply as a product of differences in personality. Person-driven revolt can have serious and unintended effects on an organization. When a group of risk agents empower themselves to bring down *a person* at any cost (rather than a policy, for example), the results can be good, but are sometimes devastating.

The final type of risk agency revolution is *transformative*. One of the central goals of the progressive leadership movement has been to empower people with the means to influence their workplace. Leaders in the classical mold, on the other hand, often fear the methods and implications of empowerment. But risk leadership assumes that neither classical nor progressive leadership is capable of producing the kind of change that risk agencies sometimes demand. Risk leaders see transformation as a means of replacing older cultures of control and stability with new, dynamic, adaptable cultures.

Risk leaders expect to encounter reluctance and resistance on the part of classical and progressive leaders when those leaders are asked to relinquish some of their control of the organization. Transformative change happens when frustration with existing organizational values and culture reaches a critical mass. The conviction that things could and should be better grows, and there

> *Transformation is a means of replacing old cultures with new, dynamic cultures.*

is a broadly-shared feeling that real change must happen or the organization will fail. Transformative change is driven by a desire to make the organization better. Risk leaders believe that the risk agency must take it upon themselves to facilitate transformative change. Such change is extremely difficult to bring about, for it is long-term, and not based on limited intervention or one or two discrete acts by the risk agency. To make transformative change happen, risk leaders must be extremely dedicated and committed to their cause. Without extraordinary determination, the process will end prematurely and outcomes will be—at the very least—unsatisfactory.

RISK AGENTS AND THE RISK AGENCY

Risk agents are unsatisfied with the performance of their organization. They are lower and middle-level employees who may or may not have great ambitions for their own careers, but are very concerned for the well-being of their unit and the organization as a whole. They are typically younger and newer to the company, and upwardly mobile. Risk agents are often viewed as energetic, enthusiastic, innovative, and—most importantly—they have a reputation for hard work and strong performance. These qualities equip them with the capacity to take the risks involved in challenging authority.

Risk agents have a deep interest in the success of their organization.

To successfully confront an organizational power structure, a single risk agent cannot act alone. Even two or three risk agents may not be able to survive in a long-term struggle against management. What is needed is a *coalition of revolutionaries* who empower themselves to challenge and transform the organization. This coalition is called a *risk agency*, and it operates from the premise of the power of many. The formulation of this larger risk agency confronts the organizational hierarchy with a new center of power that must be recognized and reckoned with. A strong coalition affords risk agents their best opportunity for success.

Informal coalitions of revolutionaries share certain beliefs in common. First, they have a strong belief that their organization or company should and could be better. Second, risk agents no longer have faith in management's ability to successfully lead the organization. They view management as having little interest in or openness to genuine transformation, and as lacking the courage to make difficult decisions. Finally, risk agents believe they can and should play an active role in shaping and improving the future of the organization. They believe that, if the organization is to grow and prosper, it will be because of their efforts.

Although risk agents are at the core of the "revolt," the risk agency also includes other persons as well. Usually as a function of the particular issue of the moment, risk agents recruit others to join them. The recruitment of *stable guard members* provides significant power and protection for the risk agency. These are employees who are considered to be organizational lifers and are seen by management as critical to the stability of the organization. They are extremely loyal, and their (stable guard members) deep knowledge of internal organizational processes makes them particularly important and useful.

Risk agencies may also seek support from outside the organization. Influential players in the larger industry can often bring credibility and strength to the cause. Finally, the selective recruitment of a few renegade top managers—usually those with a strong interest in a particular issue—can be an especially effective tactic. Such individuals bring with them crucial information, knowledge, access to resources, and therefore power.

Selective recruitment of renegade top managers can be an especially effective tactic.

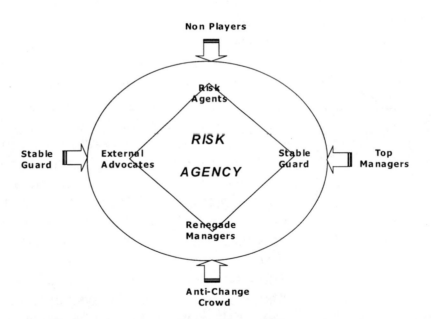

To be successful, a risk agency must bring a new player to the poker game, a player with chips too valuable for others around the table to ignore. Although the size and strength of risk agencies vary, if successful they will become a permanent force in the organizational power arrangement.

THE PROCESS OF RISK LEADERSHIP

Risk leadership sees *bottom-up empowerment* as the only real means of bringing about real change. It calls on risk agents to pressure the traditional elements in an organization to consider new and innovative solutions to organizational problems. Whether the revolt is motivated by a single issue, by problems with current leadership, or by the need for transformative change, the work of the risk agency follows three basic steps: *preparation, revolution, and resolution.*

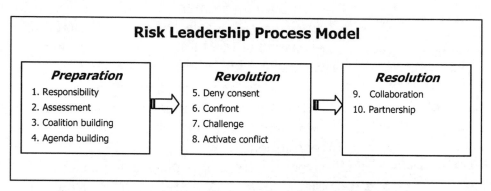

Risk agents and their coalition of revolutionaries take responsibility for making empowerment work.

First, risk agents must prepare adequately for the struggle ahead. The first part of preparation is *taking responsibility*, both for your organization and their action. Next, the risk agent *assesses the organization*. Following this, the risk agent *builds a strong risk agency*—the coalition of revolutionaries. The final part of preparation is to *develop an alternative agenda*.

Next, risk agents challenge, test, and to some degree, deny the power of management. There are limits to the power any leader exercises. Risk agents do not follow leaders blindly; rather, they *deny them unchecked power*, and the ability to make and implement decisions without accountability. Next, the risk agency *confronts* management. Here, risk agents simply say, "NO! We have a better idea!" Then they challenge authority, either directly or indirectly. Whether done behind closed doors or openly, risk agents challenge the agenda (or the lack of an agenda) proposed by management. The risk agency then recommends an alternative. The risk agency will work through the system, around the system, and at times, subvert the system to carry positive change forward. Next, risk agents will often be required to *activate conflict* in order to have their vision and plans for change adopted. Conflict is neither easy nor comfortable, but without this discomfiting strategy, management may not be willing to recognize the new power arrangement and make genuine changes.

To avert anarchy, both sides must eventually compromise. It becomes apparent to the risk agency and management that only by working together can real progress be made. Each is dependent on the other. Risk agents bring energy, innovation, and labor, while management brings needed resources to the table. This interdependence demands *collaboration*. As a final step in successfully creating and institutionalizing a risk agency, the traditional organizational culture must be modified in favor of a culture of real empowerment, innovation, and partnership. In one sense, this means the creation of a permanent revolution of sorts. But by its very nature (revolutionary, innovative, and driven by current issues), this seems to defy creating a central culture of any sort.

Risk agents must create an organizational culture that not only accepts confrontation and challenge, but also expects it.

The point is that risk agents aim to make the process of confrontation and challenge something that is expected and understood. Opposing power then becomes allowed and respected, institutionalizing an environment in which confrontation is normal and expected. For such a culture to endure, successful revolutionaries must be rewarded in each event, but a way must also be found to help unsuccessful risk agents back to their feet. Even when a risk agency fails, room must be provided for their alternative views, or factions and counter-cultures will take over where the risk agency left off, with more destructive consequences in the end.

OUTCOMES OF RISK LEADERSHIP

Risk leaders argue that organizations will not truly improve unless something more than the decision-making ability of top management is relied upon. If members truly care about an organization, they need not and should not leave decisions in the hands of the CEO and his or her small circle of lieutenants. Risk leadership assumes that transformational change cannot happen without the involvement of the rank and file. If management will not share power, the rank and file who truly care about the organization must confront and challenge the power of management. Therefore, the responsibility for success or failure rests both upon management and upon lower and middle level members. Organizational health is seen as a function of the success of energetic and innovative employees who are willing to be *risk agents*, confronting and challenging the ideas and methods that flow from traditional power arrangements.

There is greater risk in not having the will or courage to challenge the way things are done.

Risk leaders recognize the *risks* of such an approach to members, their coworkers, and their organizations, but see a greater risk in doing nothing. While the risks involved for risk agents and the organization in general are real and must be considered, traditional forms of leadership are seen as even more dangerous. Failure to risk is itself seen as a threat to the survival of an organization, because opportunities to increase productivity and collective viability are lost. Failure to risk is seen as acceptance of mediocrity and status quo thinking—acceptance of organizational structures that deny real empowerment give management unfettered control. Failure to risk is seen as saying "no" to transformation and change, and "yes" to stagnation and control.

Risk leaders believe that neither classical nor more contemporary approaches to leadership have allowed organizations to reach their potential. As a result, many organizations that should have survived did not. Neither the centralized control mandated by classical leaders nor the so-called "empowerment" espoused by top managers is seen as having the ability to take an organization as far as it could in fact go. Classical leadership is bound to slow, incremental organizational change, and progressive leaders insist on dictating and controlling processes that are in fact only pseudo-empowering. Risk leaders see progressive leadership as approaching, but in the end only flirting with, the concepts of genuine transformative change and empowerment.

RISK LEADERSHIP CULTURES

The ultimate goal of risk leadership is the transformation of the manner in which organizations empower their employees. In a risk leadership culture, empowerment comes from all levels and, more importantly, self-empowerment is expected from all employees. Such a culture accommodates the expectations of workers, not from a classicist outlook, but from a vision of workers as equal partners in a continually changing enterprise. This assumes that members see their organizations as more than "just another job." Risk cultures cannot be fostered or perpetuated if those in the culture fail to see that what they do at work can and should be a primary source of fulfillment and purpose.

> "When serving a worthwhile, creative purpose, employees can become intensely committed to [an organization's purpose]. Ultimately this is the bedrock of competitive advantage."   (Badaracco and Ellsworth, 1989)

True empowerment, however, comes at some cost, for it involves surrendering organizational control. Human organizations embrace genuine dialog and free exchange as the primary means of generating and testing ideas. Risk leadership builds upon this basic principle. Without free inquiry, a work culture will ultimately experience interpersonal failure, decreased profitability and poor workmanship. The culture of risk leadership embraces free thinking and open inquiry.

Risk culture accepts conflict as a means of resolving problems.

Risk leadership cultures also accept conflict as a means of resolving problems. Many of us are taught from infancy that fighting is "bad," and that conflict will rarely get us what we seek. As adults we are conditioned to feel guilty about making a scene or being troublemakers. Organizations, too, can effectively destroy that which is personal and human by replacing it with policies and procedures that are not to be questioned. Risk leadership does not, on the other hand, advocate conflict simply for the sake of conflict. Policies are important when they provide guidance and direction, but cannot and should not be used to eliminate ambiguity, or be seen as perfect solutions to situations. Risk cultures encourage healthy questioning of conformity as a means of making organizations better. Conflict is seen as a legitimate means of gaining the attention of management that has become entrenched in policies and procedures. Rocking the boat may be the only means to opportunities for genuine exchange.

Everyone in a risk leadership culture must take responsibility for the health of the organization; they must be accountable to it, and harbor a deep, personal commitment to its long-term success. Risk agents place empowerment over structure and people over policies. Risk leadership seeks to provide a means to genuine transformation and growth that overcomes the weaknesses of classical and progressive approaches.

SUMMARY

To implement *bottom-up empowerment,* risk agents develop a *coalition of revolutionaries* who together form a unified front that can effectively challenge management. Risk agents are members of the organization who are generally unsatisfied with its performance. They are energetic, innovative, hard working, and have deep concern for the future of the organization. Although the structure of risk agencies will vary, risk agents share three fundamental ideas: (1) they believe that the organization could and should be better; (2) they have lost faith in management's ability to lead the organization; and (3) they believe that their risk agency can play an active role in improving the organization.

The risk agency, comprised of risk leaders and their allies, represents a new locus of power that alters the organization's decision-making framework. Risk leadership sees all members at all levels as having the potential to become effective agents of organizational change.

REFERENCES

Badaracco, J. R. and Ellsworth, R. R. (1989). *Leadership and the quest for integrity.* Boston, MA: Harvard Business School Press.

Brungardt, C. L. & Crawford, C. B. (1999). "In search of true empowerment: Risk leadership theory." *On The Horizon*, 7 (3), 7-9.

Brungardt, C. L. & Crawford, C. B. (1999). *Risk leadership: The courage to confront and challenge.* Longmont, CO: Rocky Mountain Press.

Crawford, C. B. & Brungardt, C. L. (1999). *Toward a Coalition of revolutionaries: The new mandate for risk leadership.* Paper Presented at the Association of Leadership Educators Annual Convention.

Hornstein, H. A. (1996). *Brutal bosses and their prey: How to identify and overcome abuse in the workplace.* New York: Riverhead.

Chapter 10   **Name** _____

DISCUSSION QUESTIONS

1. Discuss the three things that motivate risk leaders to make the decision to act.

Reason #1 _____

_____

_____

_____

_____

_____

_____

Reason #2 _____

_____

_____

_____

_____

_____

_____

Reason #3 _____

_____

_____

_____

_____

_____

_____

2. Discuss the relationship between risk agents, the risk agency, and other organizational players. What roles do each of these groups play in the risk leadership event?

_____

_____

_____

_____

_____

_____

_____

_____

_____

3. Discuss the costs and benefits of engaging in risk leadership.

_____

_____

_____

_____

_____

_____

_____

Chapter 10   Name _____

ACTIVITY

The Risk Leadership Inventory is a self-assessment designed to measure your practice of risk leadership. Read each statement carefully and determine the choice that best corresponds with your actual behavior.

1	2	3	4	5
Rarely	**Once in a While**	**Sometimes**	**Fairly Often**	**Almost Always**

For each question, record the number corresponding to your response in the space provided.

_____ 1. I assume personal responsibility for success of my organization. (1)

_____ 2. I encourage and participate in teamwork with those who share similar beliefs. (1)

_____ 3. When I argue my position with management, the argument is based on reason and evidence. (2)

_____ 4. Despite differences, I am willing to work with management for the good of the organization. (3)

_____ 5. I am willing to both challenge and collaborate with management, even if doing so feels uncomfortable. (3)

_____ 6. Organizational improvement is my responsibility. (1)

_____ 7. Using rational arguments, I openly challenge the policies of management. (2)

_____ 8. Following management's reaction to my challenge to their power, I am able to refuse to change my position. (2)

_____ 9. I stand my ground even when management threatens punishment.(2)

_____ 10. I stand up to management when they are wrong. (2)

_____ 11. I assume personal responsibility for my work assignment. (1)

_____ 12. I actively seek out and join others who share my concerns about the organization. (1)

_____ 13. Even after management re-exerts power, I refuse to bend. (2)

_____ 14. My allies and I are unified in our concern for the collective good of our organization. (1)

_____ 15. I am not afraid to present an alternative agenda to management policies. (2)

_____ 16. I recognize the limitations and competencies of upper management. (1)

_____ 17. I actively seek consensus with my organizational allies. (1)

_____ 18. I demand that management recognize my right to confront and challenge them. (3)

_____ 19. I recognize my strengths and weaknesses as an effective organizational player. (1)

_____ 20. I am willing to engage in extended conflict with management. (2)

_____ 21. When I believe my stance is justified, I stand my ground. (2)

_____ 22. I am prepared to oppose management when I am convinced that my position is right. (2)

_____ 23. I have a good understanding of the strengths and weaknesses of my organization. (1)

_____ 24. I am willing to risk conflict with management for the purpose of making our organization better. (2)

_____ 25. Even after extended conflict, I appreciate management's value to the organization. (3)

_____ 26. I join others to create an alternative agenda for organizational success. (1)

_____ 27. I am willing to work with management to establish a common vision and purpose for our organization. (3)

_____ 28. I deny management's ability to exercise power when current policies hurt the organization. (2)

_____ 29. I am willing to continually engage in confrontational strategies to make our organization better. (3)

_____ 30. I recruit others, both within and outside the organization, to serve as allies. (1)

©1999 Brungardt & Crawford

1. To calculate your total risk leadership score, simply add your total points on all 30 questions.

Risk Leadership Score: _____.   An average score is about 90.   If you score above 120, you are a risk leader. If you score less than 60, you rarely engage in risk leadership.

2. To calculate your score for _preparedness,_ total the points only for questions with a (1) at the end.

Preparedness Score: _____.   An average preparedness score is 36.   Scores above 48 indicate strong ability to prepare for risk leadership. Scores less than 24 indicate limited ability in this area.

3. To calculate your score for _revolution,_ total the points only for questions with a (2) at the end.

Revolution Score: _____.   The revolution score can be interpreted in the same manner as the preparedness score. A score of 36 is average, 48 is high, and 24 or less is low.

4. To calculate your score for _resolution,_ total the points only for questions with a (3) at the end.

Resolution Score: _____.   An average score on the resolution section is 18. Scoring 24 or more indicates strength in collaboration, while a score less than 12 suggests weakness in this area.

CHAPTER 11

FOLLOWERSHIP

This chapter discusses new and emerging understandings of the role followers play in the leadership process. The post-industrial view of leadership is described as a "collaborative endeavor" in which both leaders and followers participate. The power that followers possess, their behavioral styles, and the five dimensions of courageous followership are presented. The concepts of servant and shared leadership are also presented.

CHAPTER OBJECTIVES

After reading this chapter you should be able to:

√ understand the changing view of followers in the post-industrial paradigm of leadership,

√ explain the critical role followers play in contemporary leadership,

√ identify the most common followership styles,

√ list the important dimensions of a courageous follower, and

√ explain servant leadership, shared leadership, and followership.

INTRODUCTION

As mentioned in Chapter 8, *The New Age of Leadership*, a notable theme in contemporary theories of leadership is the important role of followers. Older views largely failed to grasp the impact followers have on the entire process of leadership. It was traditionally believed that followers did little, and that leadership was no more than what leaders wanted and did. In leader-centered views of leadership, followers are relatively unimportant. Today, many scholars and practitioners recognize the critical role followers play with leaders in the leadership process. Because contemporary theories understand leadership as a relationship, it is necessary to consider the important contributions of those who collaborate with leaders.

Over the past twenty years, numerous books and articles have been written about followers and followership. Most of this writing has focused on the unrecognized roles, duties, and even power of followers who participate in leadership. This chapter introduces some of the most important work in this regard. First, we examine Rost's emerging view of followers, which is consistent with his post-industrial perspective of leadership. Next, Robert Kelley's (1992) five followership styles and Ira Chaleff's (1995) dimensions of the courageous follower are presented. Finally, the relationship between shared leadership, servant leadership, and followership is discussed.

EMERGING VIEW OF FOLLOWERS

Contemporary theories view followers as associates and collaborators in leadership.

Over the past century, scholars in the field of leadership have for the most part ignored the role that followers play in the leadership process. Thousands of books and articles were written about leaders and leadership with little or no discussion of followers. The working assumption was that leadership was about what leaders did, and that followers did very little—if anything—of significance. Simply put, followers did not count in traditional understandings of leadership.

Similar assumptions are still very much at work in many quarters. Consider for a moment your reasons for reading this book. Was it to learn how to be an effective leader, or because your goal is to be a better follower? People generally desire the power associated with leadership—the ability to make things happen. Followership, on the other hand, has a generally negative connotation in our society. Because leading is associated with winning, following is automatically associated with losing.

Rost (1993) believes that the industrial paradigm has much to do with this negative association. He argues that society has seen followers and followership as passive and negative because:

- average people and the ruling classes were believed to be separate and different from one another
- followers were seen as intellectually inferior and in need of the assistance and control of capable leaders
- most people were willing to give ruling classes control over their well-being
- followers were seen incapable of productivity without the guidance of leaders

Followers are increasingly recognized as playing a major role in the processes of leadership.

According to Rost, the industrial paradigm saw followers as subordinates who acted in a submissive and passive manner. Leaders were those with formal authority who acted in a directive and active way. Most scholars today take a very different view. In the post-industrial paradigm, leaders are not necessarily those with formal authority, and followers are not necessarily subordinates. In the contemporary view, followers are recognized as important associates and collaborators in leadership, and as playing a major role in the leadership process.

As noted in Chapter 8, Rost defined leadership as *an influence relationship among leaders and followers who intend real changes that reflect their mutual purposes*. If leadership is a relationship, it follows that those in the "leader" role must work beside and interact with others Rost describes the post-industrial view of followership as follows:

- *Leadership is a relationship.* If leadership is a relationship, then it is not possible for leadership to involve only the leader. One person does not make a relationship.

- *Leaders and followers intend real change.* Leadership is not about seeking changes for the benefit of the leader; rather, it is about collectively pursuing changes that are desired by both leaders and their followers.

- *Only active people are followers.* Only those people who are active in the leadership process can be considered followers. Passive people do not participate in the relationship, and thus, are not followers. They are non-players.

- *Followers can become leaders and leaders can become followers.* Sometimes we choose to lead, while at other times we may choose to follow. We are not stuck in only one role in the multiple relationships in which we find ourselves. In simple terms, in one situation we can be leaders, while in others we may be followers.

- *Much of the power in the leadership relationship rests with the followers.* If a leader's influence is based on persuasion and not on authority, then it is up to the followers to decide from whom and when, where, why, and how they will open to influence. The seeds of the leadership process are the decisions of followers to become influence receptors. The leader's role is to attempt to persuade, and the followers' role is to accept or reject that attempt. If followers lack the freedom to make that choice, then the relationship involves coercion rather than leadership.

BEHAVIORAL STYLES OF FOLLOWERS

"If the people will lead, the leaders will follow."
Robert Kelley

In his book *The Power of Followership* (1992), Robert Kelley also talks at great length about the exceptional ability of followers to lead themselves. Kelley believes that followers are responsible for more than 80 percent of the success of any organization. Without effective followers, it would be impossible for leaders to accomplish their goals. For organizations to be successful, Kelley believes it is critically important to understand followership and what distinguishes effective followers from others. Characteristics like enthusiasm, intelligence, self-reliance, and participation are especially important. In his research, Kelley identified five followership styles rooted in a pair of two-dimensional measures: independent/dependent and active/passive. The five styles are summarized below.

- *Alienated followers* are critical and independent in their thinking, but passive in their duties. They affect the organization positively because they think for themselves, play devil's advocate, and often stand up for others. Negatives are that they can be seen as being troublesome and negative, rebels without a cause, and headstrong. They usually do not support the leader.

- *Conformist followers* are dependent and seldom challenge the leader. Positives are that they easily accept work assignments, they are team players, and trust and commit themselves to the leaders and the organization. Negatives are that they lack their own ideas and are unlikely to take needed but unpopular positions when necessary. Most see them as "yes people."

- *Pragmatists* strike a balance between both the independent/dependent and active/passive scales. They adapt to the situation, stay out of trouble, and try to survive. Positives are that they get things done, keep things in perspective, and play by the rules. Negatives are that they often play political games and are always pursuing their own self-interest.

- *Passive followers* are those individuals who display none of the characteristics of effective followers. They look to the leader to do their thinking, they need constant attention, and take little initiative. According to Kelley, leaders see passive followership as a personality flaw rather than the leader's responsibility. Research tends to support the notion that the passive follower is a product of the environment rather than having a personality flaw preventing more effective participation.

Followers assume ownership, are self-starters, and use their talents and resources to benefit the organization.

- *Effective followers* think for themselves and are active organizational players. They are enthusiastic, energetic, and are seen by others as risk takers and independent problem solvers. They are innovative, assertive, and willing to stand up to the leader when needed. Effective followers assume ownership, are self-starters, and use their talents and resources to benefit the organization.

THE COURAGEOUS FOLLOWER

Ira Chaleff (1995), another scholar in the field of organizational performance and followership, has developed a series of dimensions or expectations for followers. Chaleff believes that organizations and their leaders can be successful only when followers step out of passive roles and become active participants in organizational change. His model encourages followers to be courageous and to push their leaders in positive directions. Listed below are Chaleff's five dimensions of courageous followership:

- *The courage to assume responsibility.* Active and effective followers assume responsibility for themselves and their organizations. They do not wait for leaders to tell them what to do; instead, courageous followers accept ownership and actively pursue the goals of the organization.

Effective leaders are effective followers with expertise.

- *The courage to serve.* Courageous followers are willing to work hard and serve organizational leaders. They are willing to go beyond the call of duty and accept new and challenging responsibility for the purpose of benefiting the organization.

- *The courage to challenge.* Followers must be willing to voice their discontent when they believe that things are not right. Courageous followers "are willing to stand up, to stand out, to risk rejection, and to initiate conflict" when the actions of the leader or organization are not appropriate.

- *The courage to participate in transformation.* Courageous followers acknowledge and actively pursue organizational transformation. They are willing to overcome resistance and struggle through the difficult processes of change.

- *The courage to leave.* Courageous followers recognize when it is time for them to leave. There are times when a leader's actions or the goals of the organization are not congruent with the personal principles of some followers. These followers must be willing to withdraw.

SERVANT LEADERSHIP, SHARED LEADERSHIP, AND FOLLOWERSHIP

The concept of shared (or distributed) leadership, introduced in Chapter 9, can be reconsidered in the context of followership. Shared or distributed leadership makes certain assumptions about every member of an organization:

- Every member is capable and has expertise.
- At any point, expertise can thrust a follower into a leadership role.
- Effective followers take their leadership role seriously, with the aim of helping their team or organization.
- Effective leaders are effective followers with expertise.
- The division between leading and following becomes blurred as people act according to their abilities and expertise rather than according to a title or sense of entitlement.

The post-industrial leadership paradigm embraces the idea that any given organization has not just one leader but many, each possessing special expertise. While there may be only one CEO or president, leadership is not limited to a particular number, but rather is bound only by abilities and interests. The "new" organization not only accepts shared power relationships, but also expects people to assume leadership roles whenever necessary to guide their team and organization.

The role of the leader is to be a servant, not just of the organization but of the followers as well.

Shared leadership has taken form in another approach, called *servant leadership*. Servant leadership was originated and popularized by Robert Greenleaf, but derivations of this philosophy can be found in numerous contemporary leadership writings. The basic premise of servant leadership centers around the attitudes and behaviors of the leader in relation to followers and the overall organizational mission. The role of the leader is to be a servant, not just of the organization, but of the followers as well. Servant leadership is rooted in a Biblical concept of leaders as those who serve all others (Greenleaf, 1977). As servants, leaders are best able to understand the demands and needs of an organization and its followers.

In some ways, Robert House's Path-Goal theory takes a similar approach, as leaders are to clear a path toward the goal of broader organizational success. But Greenleaf goes much further than this, suggesting that, because the leader is a model for the entire organization, he or she bears responsibility for the common good of the organization and society. In many cases, Greenleaf's ideas have been expanded to the actions of the leaders outside of their organizations in community and non-profit endeavors. Leaders should serve those in need, be they in the organizational realm or outside. The appeal of servant leadership springs from its simplicity and its spirit. Knowing that a leader is there to help a follower, rather than to direct, control, or manage an employee, changes the tone of the relationship.

Servant leadership does not offer specific guidance on how leaders can or should serve others, or on how followers should reciprocate that service, other than to say that followers serve the same common good that leaders do. Some criticize this approach for being overly philosophical, and impractical in some organizational contexts where serving everyone is not always possible or desirable.

Servant leadership and shared leadership both assume a common method for achieving their ends—collaboration. Shared leadership fails if team members cannot collaborate on a project. Likewise, serving others is impossible if there is no collaborative focus. Collaboration is the ability of people to work together to achieve a common goal that individually they would have not been able to achieve. Serving others assumes that you can work with them to achieve a broader common goal than you might have achieved working in the traditional leader-follower relationship (Chrislip & Larson, 1994).

SUMMARY

The new view of followership clearly places followers in an active role in the leadership process. Today, we no longer ignore followers and their contributions. Followers are recognized as holding tremendous power in the leadership relationship, and often as holding the keys to organizational success. This new view encourages followers to assume more responsibility, and, when appropriate, to challenge leaders and organizations. Leaders, in turn, have increased responsibility to both their organizations and their followers.

REFERENCES

Chrislip, D. D. & Larson, C. E. (1994). *Collaborative leadership*. New York: Jossey-Bass.

Chaleff, I. (1995). *The courageous follower: Standing up to and for our leaders*. San Francisco: Berrett-Koehler.

Greenleaf, R. (1977). *Servant leadership*. New York: Paulist Books.

Kelley, R. E. (1992). *The power of followership*. New York: Doubleday.

Rost, J. C. (1991). *Leadership in the twenty-first century*. New York: Praeger.

Rost, J.C. (1995). "Leaders and Followers are the People in this Relationship," *The leader's companion: Insights on leadership through the ages*. New York: Free Press.

Chapter 11

Name _____

DISCUSSION QUESTIONS

1. Discuss the view of followers under the industrial paradigm of leadership.

_____

_____

_____

_____

_____

_____

_____

_____

_____

2. Discuss in detail the new view of followers under the post-industrial paradigm.

_____

_____

_____

_____

_____

_____

_____

_____

_____

3. Describe the strengths and weaknesses of each followership style.

Alienated followers _____

_____

_____

_____

_____

Conformist followers _____

_____

_____

_____

_____

Pragmatists _____

_____

_____

_____

_____

Passive followers _____

_____

_____

_____

_____

Effective followers _____

_____

_____

_____

4. Discuss the five dimensions of a courageous follower.

_____

_____

_____

_____

_____

_____

_____

_____

_____

_____

5. List and describe at least two consistencies among Rost's, Kelley's, and Challef's ideas of followership.

_____

_____

_____

_____

_____

_____

_____

_____

_____

_____

_____

Chapter 11   **Name** _____

ACTIVITY

1. Create a profile of an ideal follower. Apply what you have learned about the various types of followers and pick what you consider to be the best attributes.

   _____

   _____

   _____

   _____

   _____

   _____

   _____

   _____

   _____

   _____

2. Now, describe a situation where you personally served as a courageous follower and challenged the leader.

   _____

   _____

   _____

   _____

   _____

   _____

   _____

   _____

   _____

LEADERSHIP AS ETHICS

This chapter discusses the relationship between leadership and ethics. This difficult and controversial topic has been heavily debated in the leadership literature, and it goes to the heart of the definition of leadership itself. Recent work has looked at the implications of viewing ethics as an essential element of leadership, and even at the possibility of reversing the equation and viewing leadership as a form of ethical expression.

CHAPTER OBJECTIVES

After studying this chapter you should be able to:

√ explain why some theorists now believe there is an essential link between leadership and ethics,

√ identify important common elements related to ethics in the work of Burns, Rost, and Greenleaf,

√ explain why leadership might logically be understood as one way of living an ethical life,

√ state a definition of leadership that incorporates ethics as an essential element, and

√ outline the difference between leadership and management on the basis of the role of ethics.

INTRODUCTION

Previous chapters have presented a number of ways of thinking about or defining leadership. But what part, if any, should ethics play in leadership? The word "ethics" can mean different things to different people, but the term as used in this chapter simply means "moral principles" or "morality," and the word "ethical" as used here is roughly synonymous with the word "moral."

What is the relationship between leadership and ethics? This question has been debated in the leadership literature for at least 25 years, but has received special attention very recently. One of the most significant recent works in this debate is leadership theorist Joanna Ciulla's 1998 collection of articles entitled *Ethics, The Heart of Leadership*. As the title implies, Ciulla and her contributors believe ethics is an indispensable part of leadership.

Linking ethics and leadership is supported by some of the most important theorists.

Ciulla's view makes some theorists and practitioners uncomfortable because it seems to imply that leaders are supposed to be moral. Despite this, a link between ethics and leadership is implied in some of the most highly-regarded, influential definitions of leadership. Such a link also offers important insights into one of the most difficult issues in this area—the distinction between leadership and management.

LEADERSHIP **AND** ETHICS

Of all of the theorists mentioned in earlier chapters, James M. Burns, Robert K. Greenleaf, and Joseph Rost are probably the most widely known, and have had the greatest influence on the study of leadership. All three lend support to the view that ethics is essential to leadership. As noted in Chapter 7, Burns believed that transforming leadership "morally elevates" both leaders and followers. Such leadership, he said, is concerned with ethical "end values" such as liberty, justice, or equality.

Rost's paradigm-altering study of leadership, reviewed in Chapter 8, affirmed the ethical principle of respect for human dignity as a moral principle guiding the leader–follower relationship. He argued that if the ethical principle of human autonomy or dignity is violated, something other than leadership is happening. According to Rost, this is because genuine leadership does not require that individuals sacrifice their integrity to be in the relationship.

For Greenleaf, too, ethics is essential. His concept of the servant leader, briefly introduced in Chapter 11, has had broad popular appeal for nearly thirty years, and remains highly influential. The success of a servant leader, Greenleaf wrote, is measured by the extent to which those he or she serves "become healthier, wiser, freer, more autonomous," and by whether or not "the least privileged in society" benefit from the leader's service. In saying this, Greenleaf combines the ethical principles of justice and liberty (as in Burns) with the principle of respect for human dignity (as in Rost).

In sum, the argument that leadership and ethics go hand in hand seems to have substantial support in the work of three of the most influential theorists in the history of the study of leadership. Numerous other scholars have similarly concluded that ethics plays a vital, indispensable role in leadership.

LEADERSHIP <u>AS</u> ETHICS

Burns, Rost, Greenleaf, Ciulla and others see ethics as an element *of* or *within* leadership. It may be more logically consistent, however, to think of it the other way around—to think of leadershlp *within* ethics (Potts, 2001). That is, to think of leadership as just one way of living an ethical life.

This is true because of what ethical principles represent. Ethical principles and systems attempt to provide answers to moral problems, and to help people live, as philosophers would say, the "good life." Ethical principles, by their very nature, apply in all settings. For example, if one claims to believe, as does Rost, in the ethical principle of respect for human dignity, then one cannot apply that principle only to certain groups of people. All people, regardless of skin color or stakeholder status, must be accorded the same respect.

If it is true that leaders must use ethics to lead, then they must be ethical in their other relationships and activities as well.

This means that the linking of leadership and ethics presents a special challenge for leaders. If it is true that leaders must use ethics to lead, then they must also be ethical in their other relationships and activities, and not just when they are functioning as a leader. If they fail to do this, they will be accused of "not practicing what they preach," and their credibility in the eyes of followers will suffer. Someone who is nice to you, but rude to the waiter, is not a nice person. A boss who cheats on his taxes or his wife will not be trusted or respected by employees. If he advocates honesty in the workplace, this will be seen only as a management technique or strategy, and not as something he truly believes in.

There are three important points here. First, the principles a leader espouses to his or her organization must be ethical, because ethics is essential to leadership. This is the argument of Burns,

Greenleaf, and Ciulla. Second, to be genuine, they must be principles the leader strives to live by at all times, not just in the presence of followers. The leadership activity of a person then becomes an extension of his or her personal ethical commitments. Finally, these principles must constrain both the *process* and the *products*—the means and the ends—of leadership. This means, as Rost asserts, that leaders must treat their followers and organizations ethically. It also means, however, that an organization's purpose must be ethical. The goals of leadership, as Greenleaf asserts, must also be ethical. This implies, for example, that leaders cannot—and do not—work for companies that produce products (or use processes) that do more harm than good.

LEADERSHIP OR MANAGEMENT?

In case you didn't notice, that last statement above has radical implications. Some would interpret it to mean, for example, that *there are no leaders* in a company that, for example, intentionally markets harmful products to minors. By definition, ethics has to do with a larger good. Activities that seek to advance the interests of one group without regard for the welfare of others are, therefore, unethical. By extension, if leadership is a form of ethical expression, those "leading" such activities could not be true leaders.

But if such persons are not leaders, what are they? The answer, simply put, is that they are managers only. This is not to say that management is a negative or unethical activity. Management in and of itself is morally neutral. In its simplest form, management seeks the most efficient means of getting from point A to point B. It is, therefore, a *tool* that is used to reach goals once those goals are specified, but it plays no role in the process of selecting goals. So, whether a company's goals are ethical or not, management skills are needed to achieve them.

> If "leadership" is viewed in traditional collective terms— in terms only of the good of a particular group—it is essentially no different from management.

If leadership and ethics are linked, those in charge are not leading if, for example, they knowingly violate the rights of employees in the name of efficiency. If leadership and ethics are linked, then when an organization ignores the good of others and seeks only to serve itself and its members—that is, it seeks only to survive and grow—leadership is absent. Those in charge *manage* the organization so as to achieve those ends, but they do not *lead*. However, if "leadership" is viewed in traditional collective terms—in terms only of the good of a particular group—it is essentially no different from management. In this sense, viewing leadership as a form of ethics helps clarify the difficult distinction between leadership and management.

REDEFINING LEADERSHIP

Leadership might be redefined as the art of guiding followers in collaborative pursuit of a mutually understood aspect of a larger good.

This line of reasoning has other implications as well. If ethics is essential, it needs to be incorporated into the definition of leadership. Leadership might be best understood, for example, as *the art of guiding followers in collaborative pursuit of a mutually understood aspect of a larger good* (Potts, 2001). This definition implies that ethics constrains both the means and the ends of leadership. It also implies that anyone, regardless of their formal position, can lead. Leadership would occur when one member in the relation causes another to see and affirm an understanding of how a given task or behavior serves a larger good. It would not require entire belief systems to be changed, but would require that some sharing of beliefs or values relative to a larger good be revealed or fostered.

In this light, what is the relationship between management and leadership? Can management turn into leadership at some point? Typical superior-subordinate relationships are only manage-ment relationships. These can be highly collaborative and highly effective, but they remain purely managerial relationships if there is no shared conception of a larger good. Management is *always* occurring, in fact, because it is a tool used in achieving any goal. If one member, however, understands his or her activity in the relation as serving both the good of the organization *and* a larger good (either through means *or* ends), a particular sort of *influence* is also at work. Leadership also begins to occur (it begins to accompany management) at the point when the other member adopts or moves toward that same understanding. It can move the opposite direction as well, from leadership to management, if the influence causes the other member to no longer believe that a larger good is being served. Influence is therefore the link—the causal factor—between management and leadership.

SUMMARY

The work of Burns, Greenleaf and Rost has led recent scholars to conclude not only that leadership and ethics are linked, but that leadership might be best understood as a form of ethical living. If such conclusions are valid, the difficult distinction between leadership and management becomes clearer. This view of leadership raises other difficult questions, however, because ethical issues are highly controversial. Many theorists are moving in this direction, however, because the arguments supporting such a shift are compelling. Leadership is more than management, and ethics seems to be the reason why.

REFERENCES

Burns, J. M. (1978). *Leadership.* New York: Harper Collins.

Ciulla, J. B., ed. (1998). *Ethics, the heart of leadership.* Westport, CT: Praeger.

Greenleaf, R. K. (1977). *Servant leadership: A journey into the nature of legitimate power and greatness.* New York: Paulist Press.

Potts, J. D. (2001). *The ethical difference: Why leaders are more than managers.* Longmont, CO: Rocky Mountain Press.

Rost, J.C. (1991). *Leadership in the twenty-first century.* New York: Praeger.

Chapter 12   **Name** _____

DISCUSSION QUESTIONS

1. Explain why some theorists believe ethics is an essential component of leadership.

_____

_____

_____

_____

_____

_____

_____

_____

_____

_____

2. In what way does Greenleaf's definition of servant leadership include ideas from both Burns and Rost?

_____

_____

_____

_____

_____

_____

_____

_____

_____

3. How does linking leadership to ethics constrain both the means and the ends of leadership? Give specific examples.

_____

_____

_____

_____

_____

_____

_____

_____

_____

4. How might linking leadership and ethics help clarify the troublesome distinction between leadership and management?

_____

_____

_____

_____

_____

_____

_____

_____

Chapter 12   Name _____

ACTIVITY

1. Ask at least three other people whether or not they think a leader's activities outside the leadership role have any connection to his or her effectiveness as a leader. Summarize the answers below. What comments surprised you?

_____

_____

_____

_____

_____

_____

_____

2. Ask at least three other people how they would explain the difference between leadership and management. Summarize the answers below. What comments surprised you?

_____

_____

_____

_____

_____

_____

_____

_____

_____

3. Explain an ethical dilemma you have experienced in your own life, whether leadership related or not. Are you content with the decision that you made? Why or why not?

_____

_____

_____

_____

_____

_____

_____

_____

_____

_____

_____

_____

_____

_____

_____

_____

_____

_____

_____

LEADERSHIP AND CHANGE MAKING

This concluding chapter discusses the relationship between leadership and the concept of change. The phases of the change process, the characteristics of change, and the barriers to implementing change are presented. Finally, personal characteristics needed to carry change forward are discussed.

CHAPTER OBJECTIVES

After studying this chapter you should be able to:

√ understand the vital relationship between change and the leadership process,

√ understand the basic concepts of change and the various contexts in which change takes place,

√ recognize the phases in a change process, and

√ identify the characteristics of those who most effectively bring about lasting change.

INTRODUCTION

Change is defined as the action of turning into or becoming something different than before.

The concept of change plays a critical role in the leadership process. Very simply, leadership is about creating and promoting change. Leaders may be subjects of change, but they are unique in that they are also the driving forces behind change. There are many types and forms of change (natural, evolutionary, internal, external). It is those efforts that are intentionally designed, planned, and desired that characterize the leadership process.

Contemporary leadership, therefore, can be defined as change-seeking and change-making. Whether the change is at the organizational, community, or societal level, it is about producing positive changes and improvements.

CHARACTERISTICS OF CHANGE

Every organization is built through the reconciliation of two opposing forces. The first, consistency and order, serve to stabilize the organization. The second, change and movement, serves to alter the organization. Both are essential to an organization's effective functioning, but change is what prevents stagnation. Change sometimes "goes against the grain," but without it, no innovation is possible and organizations succumb to inertia.

Studies of the topic of change have identified several important principles.

- *Change is a process, not an event.* Despite wishes to the contrary, change is never just a "one time shot." Each change has implications beyond what is immediately visible. Change is always based on a past and always has future ramifications. Change in one area often has a ripple effect on other parts of an organization. Change is not just an action; it is an entire process with no clear beginning or end.

- *Change is everywhere.* Change happens! All organizations and individuals are capable of change.

Every member of an organization plays a role in change.

- *Change can and does begin anywhere.* Change can happen at every organizational level and in every relationship. Change is not always top-down. In fact, top–initiated change is often reinvented at other levels to make it much more rational. Every member of an organization can play a role in change.

- *Problems necessitating change are everywhere.* Every social entity can and should attempt to improve. Change allows us to meet growing demands on organizations, communities, and society at large.

- *Learning about and adapting to change is essential.* Because change happens everywhere and all the time, successful individuals are those who learn from it and adapt to it. Much like our ancestors adapted to climatic change, leaders and followers must anticipate and adapt to organizational change.

- *There are individual and social responses.* Any given change nearly always has one or more unforeseen side effects on other parts of an organization. Whenever the steady state of an organization is disrupted, other individuals and groups will feel the effects in some way. Managing the unanticipated consequences of change is an important consideration.

- *Internal and external changes can affect anyone.* Change events outside an organization can have serious implications as well. External change that seemingly had little to do with your organization can in fact cause unanticipated problems.

- *Change can be deep or incremental, planned or unplanned.* Deep change, as popularized by Robert Quinn (1996) is the notion that real organizational improvement cannot occur apart from radical solutions. Incremental change makes small changes so to control a problem.

BARRIERS TO CHANGE

Sometimes the largest obstacle to confront is the change process itself.

Real change is hard work. Transformational organizational change does not happen unless formidable barriers and challenges can be overcome. Sometimes the largest obstacle to confront is the change process itself. Organizational theory tells us that organizations exist to provide and protect stability. Change agents in effect attempt to inject chaos into a controlled environment. Fear, denial, investments in the status quo, shortsightedness, habit, and tradition all represent barriers to meaningful change.

PHASES OF THE CHANGE PROCESS

Scholars and organizational consultants have posited a wide array of change models and strategies. These vary from simple 1-2-3 techniques comprehensive, elaborate models designed to transform an entire organization. McCarthy (1995) advocates a tight transition plan that includes describing the future state, identifying preconditions, evaluating abilities, developing a change master plan, and then communicating that plan. McFarland, Senn, and Childress (1993) propose a conflict model within which an innovation cycle interacts with resistance cycles to produce movement. Tichy and DeVanna (1990) describe a three-part drama including recognition of the need for change, creation of a vision, and strategies for institutionalizing change.

Although writings like these tend to present change as an easy, step-by-step process, things are rarely, if ever, that simple. Those who have been involved in serious transformation describe the process as a confusing endeavor filled with wrong turns, conflict, missed opportunities, and surprises.

Phases of the Change Process

- Refusal to accept the status quo.
- Creation of a vision for future success.
- Initiation of the change process.
- Sustaining the change process.

While these steps are easy to understand, they are anything but easy to carry out.

It is generally true, however, that every successful implementation of change involves four basic phases. These steps are easy to comprehend, but very difficult to carry out. First, an organization or community reaches a point at which it refuses to accept things the way they are any longer. This occurs, for example, when a group of workers or managers decide that they will no longer allow the quality of their product to be inferior to that of their competitors. The "point of unacceptability" is both the catalyst and anchor for transforming change.

The second phase involves creation of a vision for future success. A carefully-designed strategic vision provides the organization or community with a road map for change. If change is about moving from *what is* to *what ought to be*, the vision creation involves determining *what ought to be*. This could be as simple as a football team setting its sights on a league championship, or a community resolving to eliminate youth violence.

The third phase of change begins when change sponsors and agents communicate their vision and change plan to others in their organization or community. They then initiate the actual change process. Agents of change, however, must first have successfully communicated a vision and a clear process for reaching the vision. This communication process includes the identification of obstacles to be overcome and, most importantly, clearly communicating the reasons for and purpose of transformation. The way this communication process is carried out can have far-reaching effects on the level of commitment, compliance, or resistance change agents will encounter.

The communication process usually takes place in community-wide forums or company staff meetings. Change agents lay out the vision, the plan, solicit and listen carefully to feedback, and then seek commitment from change recipients. Only then the process of implementing the change plan begin.

Finally, for change to actually happen, the organization or community *must sustain the change process*. This is by far the most difficult phase. After initial excitement and enthusiasm have waned, and support from top leadership is no longer obvious, what will sustain the process? This is the phase where most attempts at change stumble. Day in and day out, change agents face endless obstacles. When those involved tire, internal resistance can gain a foothold. Once momentum is lost, change agents and change recipients alike may begin to look for an easier way, and the temptation is strong to go back to what was being done before. Only organizations and communities that maintain focus and energy through this difficult phase will successfully bring about transformative change.

> *For change to actually happen, the organization or community must sustain the change process.*

EFFECTIVE CHANGE AGENTS

Both leaders and followers must have a realistic understanding of, and deep respect for, change and the change process. Change-makers and promoters must have a genuine desire and commitment to serve others as well as to serve the particular cause they are advancing. Successful leaders must have special attributes that enable them to overcome the inevitable resistance they will face throughout the change process. Below are a few of those characteristics:

- *Knowledgeable.* Able to understand leadership, self-reflect, and think critically and holistically.

- *Civic-minded.* Possesses a sense of community and a commitment to something larger than themselves.

- *Cooperative.* Able to create, support, and nurture positive interpersonal relationships and group interaction, recognizing that successful transformation is accomplished only through a team effort.

- *Creative and innovative.* Able to find solutions, add new perspectives, and view things differently when solving complex problems.

- *Credible.* Recognizes that trustworthiness is the key to influencing and motivating others; aware that honesty is at the heart of integrity.

- *Critical.* Able to identify, evaluate and challenge basic assumptions; unwilling to accept things as they are.
- *Passionate.* Possesses a deep commitment to a cause and has endless energy to invest in transformative change.
- *Persistent.* Refuses to quit when faced with obstacles or opposition; able to sustain change and persist even when the odds are against them.
- *Risk-taking.* Able to take risks, fail, and deal with the resulting frustration.
- *Courage.* Willing to pay the price involved in transformative change.

Those who participate in leadership are change-seekers and change-makers.

SUMMARY

Change and the change process are at the core of leadership. Those who participate in leadership are change-seekers and change-makers in the organizations and communities in which they work and live. The change process includes four phases: refusal to accept the status quo, creation of a vision, initiation of change, and sustaining the movement. Successful change makers are characterized by special attributes.

REFERENCES

McCarthy, J.A. (1995). *The transition equation: A proven strategy for organizational change.* New York: Lexington Books.

McFarland, L.J., Senn, L.E., and Childress, J.R. (1993). *Twenty-first century leadership: Dialogues with 100 top leaders.* New York: The Leadership Press.

Nadler, D.A., Shaw, R.B., and Walton, A.E. (1995). *Discontinuous change: leading organizational transformation.* San Francisco: Jossey-Bass.

Rost, J.C. (1991). *Leadership in the twenty-first century.* New York: Praeger.

Quinn, R. E. (1996). Deep change: Discovering the leader within. San Francisco: Jossey-Bass.

Chapter 13   Name _____

DISCUSSION QUESTIONS

1. Describe the relationship between the concept of change and contemporary leadership.

_____

_____

_____

_____

_____

_____

_____

_____

2. Discuss the similarities and differences of implementing change at both the organizational and community level.

_____

_____

_____

_____

_____

_____

_____

_____

3. Discuss the phases of the change process:

Phase 1 _____

_____

_____

_____

Phase 2 _____

_____

_____

_____

Phase 3 _____

_____

_____

_____

Phase 4 _____

_____

_____

_____

4. List and describe the personal characteristics needed for successful change-making to occur.

_____

_____

_____

_____

_____

_____

_____

Chapter 13

Name _____

ACTIVITY

Phil Brown, the Director of Account Services of XYZ Corp, has recently come under fire for some of the policies that he created in the early 1990s. When XYZ was just starting to computerize, Phil was a first line supervisor in the Accounting Group. Phil managed a group of 15 account representatives and had resounding success when he instituted the following basic policies:

♦ Strict observation of corporate rules on socialization and breaks

♦ Mandatory work objectives per project

♦ Measurable performance improvements for each quarter

♦ Strict adherence to scheduling of meetings

The result of these policies was a marked improvement in the speed of integrating the computer system and overall effectiveness of the system. Phil was eventually promoted because of these successes, and his protégé was promoted to Phil's position. Samuel Smith was a smart guy, and had been out of college only two years. Phil felt he "trained him exactly as he wanted," and Samuel was very "in tune" with the way Phil liked the Accounting Group run.

About two years ago, Samuel attended an intensive two-week seminar on "Maximizing Employee Potential Through Communication and Empowerment". Following this seminar, Samuel took a much different approach to his workgroup. Samuel loosened up the performance requirements and allowed much more empowerment and personal growth. Samuel implemented flextime policies and saw absenteeism drop a staggering 55% in the past year. He provided open meetings and saw people interact more than ever before. Performance increases were marginal, but he could tell people enjoyed their job a great deal more.

About two weeks ago, Samuel and Phil met to go over his performance expectations for the next year. Samuel tried to take a new approach and talk about the improvements he had seen in his workgroup and how he was convinced that the whole company could benefit from his lessons. He also asked that he be allowed to develop his own objectives in line with the company vision and mission and work toward those objectives without interference. Phil "hit the roof" and ordered Samuel to immediately revert back to the original policies, because they worked and they made sense to him. Phil ordered him to change the policies back or he would "find someone that could manage these people the way they needed it". Phil has recently been in contact with Bob Fosters, an upwardly mobile member of the Computerized Account Services department, as a possible replacement to Samuel. Bob has always been a close friend of Phil's and would work hard to re-implement Phil's original policies.

1. What are Samuel's options in this situation and which should he choose?

   _____

   _____

   _____

   _____

_____

_____

_____

_____

_____

_____

_____

2. How could Samuel have changed his work group in a way that would have avoided this situation?

_____

_____

_____

_____

_____

_____

_____

3. Draw two conclusions about the change process based on the example in this case study.

_____

_____

_____

_____

_____

ABOUT THE AUTHORS

Dr. C. B. Crawford is the Vice-Provost for Academic Quality and holds the academic rank of Professor of Leadership Studies at Fort Hays State University. Dr. Crawford continues to teach graduate classes in the area of organizational leadership and information studies. Several of his articles have been published in national leadership and communication journals and he has written several books related to leadership.

Dr. Curtis Brungardt is Chairman of the Department of Leadership Studies at Fort Hays State University. He received his Ph.D. in Curriculum, Instruction, and Policy Studies from Kansas State University. Dr. Brungardt is an active researcher, publisher, and consultant in organizational leadership development. He has published more than a dozen articles and several books in the field of Leadership Studies.

Dr. Micol Maughan is an Assistant Professor of Management at Fort Hays State University. He received his Ph.D. in Social Psychology from Brigham Young University. He has consulted on various issues involving organizational behavior, management principles, and leadership. Dr. Maughan teaches courses in both business management and leadership studies.

Dr. Joe Potts, contributing editor, is director of International Student & Scholar Services at the University of Kansas. He received his Ph.D. in the History and Philosophy of Education from Kansas State University. He has published articles in leadership and intercultural theory, and a book on the role of ethics in leadership. Dr. Potts has taught courses in professional ethics, bioethics, and leadership studies.

CPSIA information can be obtained at www.ICGtesting.com
Printed in the USA
BVOW01n0258280714

360384BV00002B/3/P